Sartre's Sink

The Great Writers' Complete Book of DIY

For Jim

Though I can't for one minute
imagine you unblocking a drain
I hope you'll find inspiration
somewhere in this collection.

Yours

[signature]

Also by Mark Crick

Kafka's Soup: A Complete History of Literature in 17 Recipes

Sartre's Sink

The Great Writers' Complete Book of DIY

Mark Crick

GRANTA

Granta Publications, 12 Addison Avenue, London W11 4QR

First published in Great Britain by Granta Books, 2008

Text and illustrations copyright © Mark Crick, 2008

Mark Crick has asserted his moral right under the Copyright, Designs and
Patents Act, 1988, to be identified as the author of this work.

A CIP catalogue record for this book
is available from the British Library.

1 3 5 7 9 10 8 6 4 2

ISBN 978 1 84708 047 9

Typeset by M Rules
Printed and bound in Malta
by Gutenberg Press Ltd.

Contents

Hanging Wallpaper

with Ernest Hemingway

Tools:
Pasting brush
Wallpaper brush
Decorator's scissors
Pasting table
Plumb line

Materials:
Wallpaper
Wallpaper paste

The old man had worked for two days and two nights to strip away the old wallpaper and now on the morning of the third day the time to hang the new paper had come and he was tired. His palms were blistered from long hours scraping away the old paper and the blisters had begun to weep. The old man felt the pain in his hands as he looked again at the bare walls of the room. "Room, thou art big. But I will finish this *trabajo* that I have begun," he said. "Or I will die trying."

The old man held the line delicately in his right hand. He threaded it through the eye on the lead weight, then he made fast the end of the line to hold the weight in place. The lead weight pulled firmly now and as he let the line run through his fingers he raised his arms so that the weight did not touch the ground, and the line remained taut and straight. Now he was ready. His right hand holding the line between thumb and forefinger, the left feeding the line, the old man raised his hands and climbed the first of the steps and offered the line to the wall where it swung like the pendulum of a clock. He could feel the tension on the line as it swung and he waited patiently. "It is losing momentum, soon it will circle and stop," he thought. Then he felt the weight go still and saw that the line hung straight between heaven and earth, and the old man took the pencil from behind his ear and drew a mark on the wall beside the plumb line.

The brown wall was patched with plaster and board, and the old man drew the line from ceiling to skirting board. As he drew, he descended, step by step, but always he held the line tight to the wall. Then the old man shouldered the first roll of wallpaper and carried it to the pasting table where he uncoiled the paper, pattern downwards, on to the wooden surface. As he unrolled the paper he bent low, his arms out straight, his palms turned up, until his face touched against the surface. Then he used two pieces of wood to stop the paper from rolling up on itself, one lengthways, one sideways.

He climbed the steps again and with the tape he measured the height of the wall from ceiling to skirting board. He wore rope-soled shoes, dark trousers and an old shirt. His shirt

was patched and discoloured, and it resembled the wall. At the pasting table he loosened his sheath knife and cut the first drop three inches longer than the wall. "I would have liked to have used the long decorator's scissors," thought the old man. "But what is the use of thinking of what I do not have. I must think only of what there is." The length of paper was longer than the pasting table and the old man tied a piece of string across the legs at one end of the table and passed the end of the paper under the string to hold it in place. "I am an old man," he thought, "but I have many tricks, and I have resolution."

He had mixed his paste long before, now the old man lifted the damp cloth that covered the bucket to keep the paste from drying and began to brush the paste on to the paper. He pulled the paper level to the near edge of the table as he pasted the near edge of the wallpaper and pushed it back to the far edge as he pasted the far edge of the paper, and in this way the table stayed clean.

Now he took two corners of the paper between thumb and forefinger and folded almost two feet of the paper back on itself, keeping paste against paste, pattern against pattern, until he had made a concertina of the whole pasted length of paper. He kept the folds loose so as not to crease the paper and he felt the slime like glue slide between his fingers. He knew if he did not make the concertina, the tension on the paper would be too great and the paper would break, and he would be left holding only the two corners, like the ears of the bull he had once seen killed when he was a young man. Or worse, the paper might tear in the middle where he could not hide the join. He climbed again the steps of the ladder to offer the pasted banner to the wall. "Will the first piece stick well?" he wondered aloud. "If the first piece sticks well I will say five Hail Marys. There, it is said." The old man had no radio and often talked to himself as he worked. He pressed the paper to the wall so that its top edge was an inch higher than the wall and touched against the ceiling. "*Puta de techo*," he said, "I cannot trust you," and he thought how the ceiling did not run true and how many times he had been betrayed by the ceiling. He was wise to have used the plumb line. Then he placed the edge of the paper against the line he had drawn on the wall. The paper slid into place and the old man took the wallpaper brush from his pocket and stroked its bristles across the surface of the paper. He saw the air bubbles beneath the surface and he brushed them out from the paper until the whole drop hung as smoothly as the wall allowed. Then, high up, he tapped the bristles of the brush along the angle where the wall met the ceiling and ran the back of his knife along the recess. When he pulled the paper away from the wall again he could see the crease in the paper. "If I had the scissors it would have been easy to cut along the fold, but you haven't got the scissors," he thought. "You have only the knife and the brush, and that is enough." With the knife he cut away the narrow strip of paper that was not needed. He wiped the knife on his trousers and then threw the strip of paper over the side of the ladder, watching as it dropped to the floor below.

The old man had worked for two days and two nights to strip the old paper and three times he had had to stop to pull nails from the wall and to fill the holes left behind. Once the head of a nail grazed his brow and drew blood. Now on the third day his back ached and his legs were weak. As he stepped down from the ladder, he sank to his knees and again tapped with the brush along the join where the wall met the skirting board, and with the knife he cut away the narrow strip of paper that was left over and tossed it aside. Raising himself, he saw the paper hanging there on the wall, and how beautiful were its bands of colour against the plaster. Then he shouldered the stepladder and carried its weight the short distance to the place where the next length of paper was to be hung.

"If the boy were here he could have the next length pasted and ready," he thought aloud. "A man should not work alone." His legs and shoulders were stiff, and the pasting brush dug into the wounds in his hands. And he felt then the depth of his tiredness and the pain of life.

The old man cut the second drop longer to allow him to match the pattern. Once it was against the wall, he slid the paper until it covered the mark he had drawn on the wall so that the two edges touched each other and then he saw how the pattern continued unbroken across the two lengths of paper. The old man felt good now. He no longer thought of the pain in his hands and in his back, and he no longer thought of the treachery of the ceiling, for it was not the ceiling's fault. He thought of the beauty of the coloured paper that covered the cracks and the discoloured plaster of the wall, and he knew that the paper was his friend. "Be calm and strong old man," he said. "Wall, I respect you very much, but I will paper you before this day is over."

Bleeding a Radiator

with Emily Brontë

Tools:
Radiator key

A chill passed over me as the housekeeper led me into the sparsely furnished chamber. Such a dismal atmosphere lay within its walls that were it not for the little window through which the flurries of snow could be seen in all their icy fury, I might have supposed myself in a tomb.

"The master suffers no one to lodge here, so make no noise, and keep your candle away from the door, though you needn't worry about light at the window; he'll not go abroad this night."

I thanked the good soul, the only glimmer of kindness in the hostile gloom that obtained beneath those rafters, and bade her goodnight. I shivered still with the cold and, regretting having left the glow of the fire too soon, I lay down in the little bed and waited for the warmth to return to my limbs. Instead, I felt the cold pinch my nose and the draughts blow down about my cheeks. Looking for their source, I noted a small radiator mounted on the wall beneath the window. Benumbed to my very heart, I quit my covers and approached the device in the hope of eliciting more warmth from the radiator than I had succeeded in drawing from its owner. My fingers tingled at its touch when I found it to be as cold as a headstone and I cursed the inhospitality of the inmates.

The cold blast skirmished around my ankles, no less fiercely than Throttler, the diabolic hound that had given me such a violent welcome on my arrival and who was as much the cause of my confinement here as the snowstorm that now raged outside. Like a mourner by the graveside I stooped down in my borrowed nightshirt and ran my hand along the pipes that led to and from the radiator. I rejoiced to feel the warmth that confirmed the presence of hot water in the pipes and that I had only to open the valve for the liquid to fill the iron structure and to begin warming this room that had stood cold for I knew not how long.

Outside the storm had increased in violence and the branches of the fir tree now set up a violent tapping at the window. Shivering, I grasped the grey knob to the left of the headstone and, not without effort, turned it counterclockwise. Scarcely had I begun opening the valve than there came an infernal knocking from beneath the floorboards, as though a host of demons were come to drag the residents of the Heights down to eternal fires. I believe I would have gladly gone with them, in the hope of warmer lodging than I had found here under Mr Heathcliff's roof.

Not wishing the housekeeper to be punished for her charity, I closed the valve and heard the violent knocking

subside. Though she had, indeed, asked me to keep my lodging in this room a secret, she could hardly have intended for me to freeze to death in its keeping, and deciding that my host and his satellites were long overdue a lesson in hospitality, I reopened the valve and heard the pipes renew their fiendish lament, as though all the dead of the moor were beating on the lids of their coffins in demand of freedom, outdoing even the howling of the wind and the tapping of the fir trees.

The drumless tattoo notwithstanding, I now felt some warmth dispersing through the white ironwork, as if a genie had been released from its lamp, though such warmth as there was failed to spread, held back, I surmised, by the presence of air trapped in the system. I cursed myself for setting out on the moor without a radiator key in my pocket, and resolved that since I could no longer hope to keep secret my occupancy of the chamber, I might as well descend to the kitchen, where I hoped to find the necessary tool in the confines of a vast oak dresser. I took up my candle and walked out into the corridor, taking care to close the door as I left.

The orchestra that was making such a noise in my room now found its accompaniment in the quarters below. Where earlier I had left my hosts sitting in silence, staring like automatons into the flames, I was now witness involuntarily to a scene of such unspeakable frenzy that I pinched myself and rubbed my eyes from disbelief. Joseph, his face blackened with ash, was fallen to his knees, beating himself about the face and head, while his master, like the devil himself emerging from the coals, stood before the fire, his arms aloft, his chest bared, howling like a wolf beneath a full moon, "Cathy, my Cathy, I hear you knocking. She is there, Joseph, she is come back." The dogs joined briefly in the baying of this mad pack, until silenced with a kick by their master as he headed for the stairwell where I now stood in my nightshirt. That old Pharisee, Joseph, followed, his hands clasped about his Bible like a miser's round his purse, as he called aloud to all the saints his credentials as a God-fearing Christian. Trembling, for cold, in all my limbs, I expected no exchange of civilities as they passed and none came. The two brutes scarce gave me a glance as they hurried by, as though summoned to the final judgement. Within moments all previous scenes of madness were forgotten. My demonic host flung open the door I had just closed and, in an uncontrollable passion of tears, began calling to every corner of that chamber for his Cathy. "See, she is here, she knocks. Come in, Cathy. Oh, Cathy, forgive me and come home."

I could no more dream of stepping back into that room had the house been in flames, than I could think of intruding on such a gush of grief and superstition. Profiting from the commotion, I continued downstairs where the kitchen of Wuthering Heights was bathed in an eerie red glow. A fine red fire illumined the chimney, and the cur, Throttler, and an Irish terrier called Djinn, accustomed to the ravings of their master, were curled up asleep on the flagstones, confirming that even the dogs of the house were not kept as short of warmth as its guests. Immediately I began to search the drawers of the old dresser, making as little noise as possible. A cold draught now reached down also into the penetralium and I guessed that Mr Heathcliff had thrown wide the window of my chamber and was calling his plea to the storm. "Cathy, come back, my love, my Cathy." Hurrying my search, I pulled open a drawer full of knives and mixing spoons. Rattling through its contents I came upon the object of my search, a small brass T-shaped key that sat shining in the cup of a serving spoon. No sooner was it in my hand than the hair rose on my neck and I froze. Behind me I heard the deep, loathsome rattle of Throttler's growl. Like a sound rising from the Underworld, its profound baritone might have made the room shake if my legs did not already shake so from the cold. The beast had me backed against the dresser and, not for the first time, I was beginning to regret crossing these wretched moors to further the acquaintance of my landlord. As the hairy monster began to pull on my nightshirt, shaking his head as though in violent disagreement at my presence, I saw in the shadows the mistress of the house, watching my discomfort as motionless and mute as had she been contemplating a kitten toying with a mouse. "Madam, I should be glad if you would call your dog off." At a gesture from her slender hand and a sharp call, the little terrier leapt up from the hearth and trotted over to rest his head on his mistress's knee. "I meant rather the dog who has hold of my nightshirt," I hastened to add.

"That. That is not *my* dog," she observed scornfully, caressing the little tawny head and looking for all the world as though the madness that currently held dominion over the household were an everyday amusement. "Were you looking for a knife?" she asked with a note of hope in her voice.

"I was looking rather for a key . . ." I struggled to remain on my feet.

"To his room? Have you come to kill him?"

Horrified, I assured the lady of the house that I had no such notion.

"You would have more chance with a knife."

I looked and saw that my hand still clutched a large wooden serving spoon, but before I could better explain my presence in the kitchen, a great bellow came from the upper regions of the house and distracted him of the tireless jaws, so that the creature momentarily loosened its grip on my borrowed nightshirt. Sensing the time had come to make my escape, with a cry of "Fetch", I threw the spoon into the shadows, tore myself free and ran. Mounting the stairs two at a time, I rushed headlong into the little chamber in which Mrs Dean had earlier wished me a pleasant night's rest. Such a sorrowful sight now met my eyes that, extraordinary to report, I forgot my pursuers and stopped still in my tracks. Mr Heathcliff, in an uncontrollable passion of tears, was kneeling beside the bed, from which I had so lately risen. "Look. Look. Her little body has lain here. Oh, see how she has turned down the counterpane." He was holding the pillow to his cheek, soaking it with his tears, "Hear me this time. Oh, Catherine, let me touch your hand. Lay down your blessed cheek once more on this pillow, that I might look upon you. Oh, my darling."

Beneath the window Joseph cited from the scriptures, calling heaven and all its angels to protect him from demons and witches, and to strike down evil-doers.

My indecorous arrival into this strange sermon had a dramatic effect. Eyes wide, the two men looked up, their gaze at first coming to rest on the great rip that scarred my nightshirt. Mr Heathcliff, seeing my eyes move, with a look of guilty authorship, from the pillow he held pressed to his cheek, to the turned-down bed and hollowed mattress, saw immediately his error. All this must have passed in the blink of an eye, for all at once I fell to the floor. With all his weight,

Throttler had struck me in the back and now, his great forepaws planted in my shoulder blades, his abominable snorting ringing in my ears, he took up guard, pinning me to the floor. Unmindful of all this, his master rose to his feet, let fall his arm to his side and dropped the white tear-stained pillow to the floor. That old zealot Joseph closed his Bible and made to stand, his brow corrugating in disapproval, as he leant his hand against the radiator.

The two men seemed unmindful of the snarls and barks with which the hounds kept me in such an embarrassing and disagreeable position and they now made to leave the room, stepping over me, as though I were no more than a tussock on the moor. As he passed, Joseph thrust out his evil tongue in expression of his peevish displeasure. "The Lord help us! It's bonny behaviour, sneaking around o't neeght, heating the place like a furnace and making paupers of us all." More of his sermon I could not distinguish, but, had I not been held fast, I believe I would have kicked the aged rascal out of the door. I hemmed and called after my surly host, "Mr Heathcliff. The dogs. If you please."

He looked back and seemed to see for the first time the hound whose huge purple tongue hung slavering on my shoulders as his fangs clasped the wooden mixing spoon. "How dare you. Under my own roof. God confound you, Mr

Lockwood. They won't meddle with persons who touch nothing. Throttler, Djinn, come away!"

I felt the four-footed fiend step from my back and, hearing the sound of the dogs' paws following the two men down the staircase, I struggled to my feet. The events of the evening had gone some way to warming me, but still too cold to sleep, I drew near the radiator. Though the lower portion was now quite hot, its upper reaches remained as cold as before, confirming my earlier supposition that there was indeed air in the system. I had not let go of the key in the pursuit and I now put it to good use, loosening the little square valve that protruded like a bolt from the upper corner of the radiator. Scarcely had I given it a half-turn than I heard the rushing sound of escaping air. I remained in that attitude for nearly a minute, waiting for the first sounds of water bubbling as it reached the valve, whereupon I tightened it at once. The transformation was almost immediate. The whole device now seemed to glow with a benign and agreeable warmth, so that I retired not just then, but gathered my pillow from the floor and drew myself upon a chair to better feel its benefit. So I nodded drowsily, contemplating the ghost of my predecessor and wishing for her as sound a sleep as I now hoped for myself, while thawing my legs on what might well have been the first warmth felt in that room for nearly twenty years.

Reglazing a Window

with Milan Kundera

Tools:
Hammer
Putty knife
Tape measure

Materials:
Glass cut to fit
Putty
Panel pins

All governments oppose transparency. They oppose it because they know that with transparency comes fragility. Such is the nature of glass. Windows can certainly be made from materials more flexible or less brittle than glass, but what is required more than anything of a window is that it is transparent. All other qualities become secondary, from which Tomas deduced that transparency creates fragility.

The crack in the pane seemed to Tomas the first sign that the fortress he had so lovingly constructed was no longer impregnable. All his adult life he had maintained between himself and the outside world an invisible barrier through which no one was allowed to pass. When he believed that he could keep her at a distance like all the others, Odile had found a way through, and the broken window proved finally that Tomas had been deceiving himself.

Before their first night together she had called to say she was staying at a hotel nearby. She was wet through when she arrived at his apartment; the city was in the grip of a storm and her eyes looked out through the long hair plastered to her flushed cheeks, like a child's from the bulrushes. Her cheek and chin were bleeding as she stood in the doorway; breathless, she described how in trying to outrun the storm her heels had slipped on the cobbles. He cleaned her wounds, found her fresh clothes to wear and wrapped her hair in a towel, while she stared at him with eyes of love that he mistook for madness. In the morning he collected her bag from the station; there had been no hotel.

The rules of Tomas's fortress did not allow a woman to stay overnight, but the doelike creature that had come to him, wounded in the storm, crossed his drawbridge unchallenged. Five days later the guards awoke to the danger. An old girlfriend was leaving the city, so Tomas took possession of her flat in the building opposite his own and installed Odile there. Now, seven months later, he stood in the little apartment and surveyed the scene. In the lounge every windowpane bar one was cracked, as if fractured by the vibration of Russian tanks entering the city through the streets below. In the bedroom every pane bar one was intact,

this last cracked as though a single white dove, thrown off course in a storm, had flown into the building. He knew then that she had been spying on him.

Sitting on the mattress that served Odile as a bed on the nights he did not permit her to sleep with him, Tomas contemplated the broken pane. In places the putty, grown old and brittle, had fallen away and he could see that the nails that had first been used to hold the pane in place had now rusted. He opened the French windows that overlooked the courtyard to remove the broken fragments that lay in the little recess below the window, and it was then, looking back into the apartment, that he saw Odile's camera, set on its tripod, like an invitation awaiting a guest. When finally Tomas gathered his courage to look through the eyepiece he discovered that the double fracture was aligned like the cross hairs of a rifle sight on his own apartment. Of the unlit interior only the area closest to the window was visible and Tomas searched his memory for any incident involving any other of his mistresses that might have been witnessed by Odile. In the lounge the same sequence was repeated: a low three-legged stool was so positioned that looking through the single unbroken pane from such an oblique angle his gaze was directed once more on to the window of his own apartment. And in that moment he recalled Tereza, cross-legged in only her panties as she sat on the chopping block by the kitchen window. She had lingered in the window, describing to him the brightness of the constellation of the Plough in the night sky, and Tomas, remarking that it was the constellation most favoured by Goethe's hero Werther, had then his first presentiment that something awful was about to happen.

Odile had left the apartment early that morning. She knew exactly what she must do. She took great care as she passed the glazier's shop in case she should meet Tomas. She had been precise about what time she wished him to arrive at her apartment. But Tomas was rarely on time and she did not want to look into his eyes and feel her resolve evaporate, so she hurried, her elegant legs dancing and leaping across the paving slabs so lightly that she seemed carried on the morning breeze. In the café a young man rose from his table to greet her, his eyes aflame, as his hungry lips and eyes fell on the offered cheek and downturned lids of the woman before him.

Tomas handed the piece of paper to the glazier. He had measured exactly the recess of each broken pane and told the glazier to reduce the size sufficiently so that the glass would fit easily. The glazier held the small shard that Tomas had brought with him and chose glass of the same weight and thickness. While Tomas searched for putty, pins and a putty knife he listened to the glass cutter's blade as it screeched across the slippery surface. Each traverse ended with the loud crack of ice breaking under heavy feet. Holding the fragile panes, wrapped in newspaper, under his arm, Tomas returned to Odile's studio.

The last debris brushed from the frame, Tomas put in the first pane of glass. It sat comfortably in its new place and he inserted one of the small nails into the top of the frame and tapped it gently with the hammer until it seemed it would stop the pane from falling. He put two more pins along each side of the pane and a final one against its lowest edge. His anxiety for the absent Odile had not completely subsided. For her every moment spent away from Tomas was time lost and he wondered again at the strange alignment of chair, pane and the window of his apartment, and breathed in the heavy linseed scent of the freshly opened putty. He felt the oiliness on his fingers and the rubbery fleshlike consistency of the clay. He tore off a lump between forefinger and thumb, and began to knead and shape it. He thought of Odile, that simple faunlike creature who had arrived from the provinces clinging to the only book she owned. How confident she now was. He had found her the job in the bookshop, introduced her to the theatre, to concerts, to his friends (not all). How much he had taught her, how much he had shaped her. The pane moved and he hammered in another nail to make clear what the balance of power was between them. Then he pressed a lump of the putty into the edge of the windowpane, pressing it firmly into contact with the glass and the wood, and continued to do so with little balls of the putty no more than the thickness of his thumb, overlapping each over the next to ensure a waterproof seal all round the window. Then he sat back down in Odile's chair and looked out across the courtyard. A movement in the window of his own apartment caught his eye. Hurriedly his eye sought for the eyepiece of Odile's camera and, as his greasy fingers fumbled to adjust the focus, his stomach began to rumble. A ray of sunlight bouncing off a window somewhere was illuminating the kitchen and there, her back against the window, he saw the long dark hair of Odile. Dressed only in her underwear she was perched by the kitchen window, on the old butcher's block that served as a work surface. Tomas's stomach rumbled again; his fingers, held so close to his face, filled his nose with the smell of the window putty. He watched the spectacle with the silent concentration that few professors ever see on the face of a student. Then Odile slowly turned her face towards him. Whether she could see him watching he did not know, but he knew this spectacle was intended for him. There was no sign of triumph on her face, nor of love, nor was it the look of hope and desire that he saw whenever he made love to her, but the look of a member of the Greek chorus who seeks to bear witness. Then the fingers of a man's hand pulled her face away and he saw that she was not alone.

When Pushkin accused Georges d'Anthes of being the lover of his wife, the two men fought a duel. Tomas, feeling for the first time since his childhood the pangs of jealousy, lunged forward to snatch up the putty knife, but Tomas's passion was not Pushkin's, so he began to cut and shape the putty round the pane, all the while trying not to think of Odile at the window. The cracked pane had been replaced, but the blow dealt by Odile had fractured more than just a pane of glass, the crack extended way beyond the confines of the window frame, an expanding fault line sapping power throughout his whole world.

Replacing a Light Switch

with Elfriede Jelinek

Tools:
Screwdriver

Materials:
Light switch fascia

Electricians are expensive, says Mother. They will take our money to stand around drinking tea. All tradesmen are wolves and women are their natural prey. They will arrive, still picking the remains of their last victim from their teeth. The tradesman, pulling his lips back to bare his fangs, will make a sucking noise. The job is not so simple, a call will have to be made, materials must be bought. Who did this? The work of the last tradesman must be put right. Have you been having a go yourself? It's a total abortion. But he can put it right; at a price.

Mother and child would have to let a cuckoo into their nest, a man who will look over the goods on offer as though *he* is the buyer. Mother would need Rosa's sharp eyes to watch the tradesman's quick hands, to check that he does the work for which he is paid, to see that he is not undoing good work to put it right again, at a price. But the mother pig does not want to let in a wolf when her little piglet is at home. Mother is only an old woman, her sight is weak from watching over her little one.

Replacing a Light Switch

Tradesmen have quick eyes, their gaze falls like fingers, touching everything, evaluating what the two women have to give. Is that an antique chest? It must be worth a few bob. A nice part of town, not cheap around here. Eyes like hands poring over the inventory: crockery and cushions, paintings and silver plate, breasts and buttocks. A tradesman will ask to use the lavatory, prying to see what underwear hangs over the bath; this way he can take stock. What kind of goods are stored in the apartment? Young ones? Old ones? Young ones are best. Some little pigs even wear underwear that says eat me up.

Rosa is perfectly suited to this kind of electrical work, her dexterous fingers fit in small spaces, her sharp eyes are used to looking at lines and symbols, clefs and crotchets. She will never have to do this work in their new flat, there everything will be new, perfect. But this old place is rotting like a corpse, they can't be wasting money on it now. Rosa gives her money to her mother, that way it can be kept safe with their savings. Mother will look after it, for now Rosa needs only a few pennies, for the bus and the tram. It is foolish to give away their hard-earned money, Mother's money, Rosa's earnings, for a simple job they can do themselves. Rosa will do the job, Mother will tell her how.

Has she turned off the power? Mother asks again and again. Her Rosa is precious and must be kept safe, so that

one day, if she is not handled roughly, she may become an antique, priceless and pristine because her drawers have never been opened. Has she removed the fuse? Has she turned off the switch?

Rosa undoes the screws on the faceplate of the switch; there are two of them. The new faceplate must be the same size, otherwise they will have to replace the existing box and then she will have to return to the electrical shop to queue among the leering men, to have them brush against her in the queue, to smell their beery, sweaty smell, to be called their darling when she is no one's darling, except Mother's.

Don't lose the screws, says Mother, they will fit back in the same holes. Mother is anxious about fitting screws in holes, she fitted a screw in a hole once and now she has Rosa, and look how much extra work that created for Mother. Years and years to put things right, now they are happy. She sent the tradesman who did that job away. He expected more than a cup of tea. Now he is discarded and Rosa remains the only evidence of his work, but not really, says Mother, any tradesman could have done the same, it is all Mother's work, his part was nothing, a clumsy blow from a hammer, a turn of the screw, a whirr of the power tool, and then he was gone.

Rosa lifts the faceplate away from the box, but strong wires hold the two together. Black and red, yellow and green. Live, neutral, earth, Earth, mother, child. Live and neutral are held together in the same sheath, they are always together, like mother and child. Mother is live, Rosa is neutral. But really Mother is the switch; she tells Rosa when to come on when to go off. Rosa is like a current that Mother controls, for her own safety, for Mother's safety. The fascia panel hangs from the cable like a child hanging from the umbilical cord; it can never be cut or the child will die, the mother will die. One after the other Rosa loosens the screws and pulls the wires free; now she can discard the old cracked control; disconnected it is useless.

The switch is serviced by a two-core and earth cable. The wires are all cocooned together in the plastic sheath. The earth conductor is still connected to the terminal at the back of the mounting box. The red and black conductors must be connected to the new switch. That's what Mother demands. You strip the wire, then you push it into the hole, where you screw it up tight so the wire cannot escape and other wires cannot enter. The back of the faceplate is marked top so that you cannot put it on upside down. This way the switch is down when the light is on and up when the light is off. It could work just as well upside down but that is not how things are done. This way Mother can always tell if the light is on or off. Rosa would like to put it on upside down, but Mother won't allow it. Use sticky tape to mark which wire goes where, snaps Mother, but there are only two wires, and they can be connected to any terminal. If there were more, Rosa could have disconnected them one at a time or marked them with labels, but that is not necessary.

Rosa removes the little screws, like grubs dormant in their holes, and pulls the wires loose. Mother is anxious; as long as the wires hang loose she is worried for her little treasure; she does not want to see her treasure electrocuted. Rosa inserts the wires into the terminals of the new faceplate and returns the screws. The holes won't be open for long, soon they will all be shut up tight, like Mother's and Rosa's, that way nothing can get in and make sparks. A short circuit would mean that Mother would no longer control the switch and that would be dangerous.

Rosa screws the faceplate back in place. Its single ivory key awaits a virtuoso's touch, not a heavy hand. No man will flick this switch. Rosa replaces the fuse and switches the power back on. See, there was no need to let a man into the house to prod clumsily at their switch with his dangerous tool. Now brave Mother can be the first to test the switch. When her finger touches the key the light goes on, and when she presses it again the light goes off. That is how she likes it.

Painting a Room
with Haruki Murakami

Tools:
5" emulsion brush
Emulsion roller (optional)
2" gloss brush
Filler knife

Materials:
2.5 litres white emulsion
5 litres blue emulsion
2 litres white gloss
Sugar soap
Sandpaper
Filler

I was twenty-three when I fell in love for the first time, a love that nearly killed me, like a volcano that draws villagers near to its fertile slopes, then covers them with ash, preserving them in a kind of frozen animation for thousands of years, except I survived to tell the tale and my internment didn't last a thousand years, not quite.

I had just graduated from the Kobe School of Journalism when I moved to Tokyo. I knew a few people there but the first friend I made in the new city was Aoko. She occasionally worked as a hostess in a well-known jazz club in the Shinjuku district. I would go there and make a whisky last all night, avoiding talking to anyone and losing myself in the music. When one day I recognised her shopping in a record store, I invited her for coffee. Over time it became a regular event and gradually she told me about herself, how her boyfriend, Toru, had killed himself the year before in his car; how her father had recently passed away after a long illness; how she had once studied the piano but could now no longer bear to touch one. She had just found a new apartment; it was in a run-down part of town but the landlord had offered a great price, as long as Aoko cleaned it up herself.

Aoko – her name meant blue – was wearing a white coat, tied at the waist, her long hair reached almost to the table top, she looked good, even under the fluorescent lighting. I had made money to put myself through college by decorating other people's houses and offered to help. She looked good enough that I would have offered, even if I had never seen a tin of paint. That time she refused, but a few months later, when I saw her again in the jazz club, she asked if the offer was still open. She still looked great and it was.

The boxy room had been given up on so long ago that we couldn't even date the décor. We cleared the room of Aoko's few belongings and together pushed the bed into the middle of the room. Aoko, dressed in a pale blue cotton shirt and

cut-off jeans, used masking tape to fix plastic sheets along the skirting boards at the edge of the floor, while I used the heavier cotton dust sheets to cover the furniture in the middle of the room.

The first task was to wash the years of grime from the walls, ceiling and woodwork. I filled a bucket with warm water and sugar soap, and, wearing purple rubber gloves I'd got from a temporary job in a pharmaceutical company, we began washing the room from top to bottom. Old cobwebs and dust were thick in the corners, and we were soon soaked with water and sweat. Judging from the yellow colour of what must have once been white, the previous resident had smoked about a hundred cigarettes a day, but the sugar soap cut through the dirt and grease as the two of us worked our way down from the ceiling to the floor. I looked across at Aoko standing on the steps so she could reach up into the corners, her right arm moving back and forth with the sponge as though she were waving to someone invisible beyond the wall. As her arm moved her body swayed elegantly, her slim hips hugged tightly by her cut-offs. My imagination kicked in and I thought of her body, naked against mine, but that happy outcome, if it was ever to occur, was still some way off in our story. When we had finished with the washing the room looked almost as if it had been repainted already. Who would believe so much stuff could cling to a vertical surface, but two buckets of dark, grimy water showed how much the years had deposited on the walls of this small room.

I had finished my side of the room and left off working. "Hey, Aoko, do you have a telephone? I need to make a call." She called me over to the window and pointed to a call box just below in the street. "What if someone wants to call you?"

"I don't give the number out much, but if I'm dressed and ready I can make it to the payphone in fifty-two seconds."

After the call I went for coffee, doughnuts and cigarettes. When I came back Aoko was admiring our work. I handed her a coffee. She said thank you. We sat on the top of our stepladders. Her slim hips, almost prepubescent, fitted comfortably into her lofty seat.

"Stopping for doughnuts and coffee is the best bit," I said. "Admiring your own work while you sit back and relax. At every stage there's something new to admire and enjoy. We'll start filling and sanding next."

"You're amazing, Yuri, I wouldn't have a clue about any of this stuff. I would have just started putting the paint on."

"Well, you could have, most people just want to get to what they think of as the best bit, but on top of all that grime it would soon have started to peel off."

I went into the kitchen to mix some filler. The kitchen

was even worse, it smelt of fat and it looked like a murder scene. I poured some of the grey-white powder into a bowl, added water and then mixed until it was like rice porridge. The filler was going to cover all the small cracks and holes that we could find. Over the years so many pictures had been nailed up in the room it looked like a mouldy cheese. I divided the mixture into two lots and with filling knives we started to give the walls back their youth, filling the wrinkles and pockmarks until the wall was peppered with dashes of white filler.

"Hey, Yuri, I'm not sure I've got the hang of this. I can't seem to get a smooth finish with this knife."

"Don't worry," I said. "We'll use sandpaper when it's dry."

As she concentrated on her work Aoko held her tongue in the corner of her mouth. I watched her, wondering how her tongue would feel on mine. She noticed I'd stopped work and pulled her tongue back into her mouth.

"Hey, I'm going faster than you."

"Not for long," I said, but I couldn't forget that tongue.

By now the ceiling and walls had dried, and we could start to paint the ceiling, brilliant white. Aoko wanted to use the paint roller. "Well, it's faster but it sends little specks of paint everywhere and the colours never look as bright. But go ahead if you want to try it," I said. While Aoko rolled the paint on to the middle of the ceiling I painted the corners and edges with a large brush. Above us the ceiling grew whiter, while the furniture, draped in white sheets, lay like a winter landscape below, and we two hovered in between like winter birds on the wing. When finally I had to descend to change the music, I took off Bill Evans's "Waltz for Debbie" and put on "Kind of Blue". From below I watched Aoko, her movements elegant and economical, her balance perfect at the top of the steps. I looked up in awe.

We knew the ceiling would need two coats but for now we waited for it to dry. Aoko put a Marlboro between her lips and the two of us took a break, the smoke rising in time with the piano towards the white of the ceiling; already its brilliance was under assault. I found a bottle of Courvoisier in the next room and poured two glasses.

"You drink brandy in the morning?" Aoko looked surprised.

"I try not to drink anything stronger before midday."

She laughed. "You're crazy, Yuri." She took the glass and her lips touched its rim with all the impact of a butterfly landing on a flower. I wondered how it would feel to have that butterfly land on my mouth and watched her nose wrinkle as she sniffed the aroma of the cognac.

"You're not trying to get me drunk?" she joked.

"I thought about it." I was honest.

I'd been with a few girls since I'd known Aoko, but it was pointless. Other relationships were like games of Russian roulette. I could sleep with them a few times, if the revolver fired on an empty chamber it was fine, but sooner or later the chamber that contained my feelings for Aoko would click into place and then blam, a bullet to the brain and it was game over.

Once before I had succeeded in getting Aoko drunk. We were sharing a cab on the way home when she forgot herself and kissed me on the mouth, two butterflies collided and finally I understood chaos theory. The resulting tidal wave crashed through my world, sweeping everything away. When the tide fell back it took everything with it and the emergency services couldn't get to me.

I had been watching Aoko for too long now without speaking. She picked up a piece of sandpaper. "Hey, Yuri, how do they make this stuff? Is it really sand?"

"Sure, there are teams working in the Gobi Desert. First with brushes they paint glue on to huge sheets of paper and then gangs of Gobi people lay the paper face down on the sand so that it sticks. If you look carefully, sometimes you can see little pieces of camel shit." Aoko laughed and gave me that cute look that said she couldn't be taken for a fool. The old balance was returned, good old Yuri. "I expect the filler's dry enough now. Let's rub it down, but use the fine paper, we'll use the rough stuff they make in Arizona for the woodwork."

The shooshing sound of sandpaper on plaster filled the room and a fine white powder settled on everything, dusting Aoko's black hair with icing sugar, collecting on eyelashes and lips; we were rapidly ageing together in a room covered with white sheets and it reminded me of a character I had once read about in Dickens. Somehow Aoko looked just as beautiful. Her whitening hair was tied back and she had on a pair of white gym shoes. She had good technique, a light touch that left each area beautifully smooth. While I sanded the door frame, skirting board and windows I watched her through the dust as she reached up to sand a patch that we'd filled high on the wall, her cotton shirt stretched taut over her breast revealing the shape of her nipple. Desire weighed in my trousers like a rock. The urge to take her in my arms was now almost overwhelming and the shooshing had become the sound of my blood rushing in my ears.

I stood behind her, kidding myself that I was looking at the work. You can only kid yourself for so long and I reached out and placed my hand on the back of her neck; her hair felt soft and smooth against my palm.

"That's enough," I said. Aoko froze, facing the wall, her hand still in its raised position; her hips were just a few inches from mine and I could feel the warmth coming from her body. I moved closer, my face level with her perfect ear, the scent of her sweat and perfume mingling with the dust. We stayed like that, immobile, listening to each other's breathing. Now that the sanding had stopped the sound of Coltrane playing "How Deep Is the Ocean" could be heard again. It was deep. I reached my left hand around her body and laid it on her breast.

Aoko was the first to speak. "Yuri san, you are my best friend, but I cannot be your girlfriend." She twisted round to face me, her face bowed; a tear ran down, leaving a glistening trail on the geisha whiteness of her cheek. I said nothing. I felt sick with myself.

"I am sorry, Yuri." Her face was still bowed. "I am not a good person for you. I will make you unhappy and I never want to do that to you. I am not as balanced as I seem and I don't want thoughts of me to hold you back. Find a nice normal girl to be your girlfriend. If you fall in love with me we can no longer be friends."

"I'm not going to kill myself, if that's what you're afraid of." I regretted it as soon as I said it. Outside the rain had begun to fall, and I thought of Toru putting his foot down on the gas and driving himself all the way to the other side, while still in neutral.

"I need to go out. Did you say we need some more gloss paint?"

I needed to go out too and stand in the rain, but Aoko had beaten me to it. "Yeh, one more litre of white gloss for the doors." I didn't try to stop her. The door closed with a click that sounded like the full stop on a vintage typewriter.

I drank another brandy and smoked a cigarette. Had I made a mistake? At the time I thought so, but now, nearly twenty years later, I'm not so sure. It didn't take me long to paint a second coat of emulsion on the ceiling and then I opened the paint for the walls: powder-blue, Aoko had chosen the colour. I stirred the liquid with a stick and then, using the wide emulsion brush, began painting the edges and corners of the room. Concentrating on the brushstrokes cleared my mind. The frame of blue that outlined the room looked so nice I could have left it that way. Aoko was taking a long time, but I guessed she needed some space. I might even have the walls painted by the time she got back. A few hours later the first coat was finished. It looked great. Light patches showed where we had used the filler but they would disappear under the second coat. It was getting late and I stopped for something to eat. I found some noodles and miso soup in the kitchen, and ate looking out of the window at the endless April rain. Where was Aoko? Why was she taking so long? By nightfall I had painted a second coat and finished the brandy. I eventually passed out on Aoko's bed, everything in the room still covered by the white dust sheets.

It was some weeks before I heard from Aoko again. I carried on living in her apartment, even after I had finished all the painting, but I left the sheets over everything, as if she had just left the room. I brought a few things from my own place but I didn't like to leave for long in case she called or showed up. One night I was woken by the sound of the telephone. I knew it was Aoko. I slept in my clothes just in case. Running through the wet street, my breathing fast and tennis shoes sliding, I made it to the receiver before the ringing stopped. On the other end of the line I could hear cars driving through wet streets. No one spoke but I knew it was Aoko. Was she holding the receiver or was it just hanging there picking up the sound of the street? At least it was raining there; we were standing in the same rain. My head leant against the glass as I looked out at the passing headlights. I told her about the apartment and how good the blue looked. "When you get back we can decide where to hang your Blue Note posters." I carried on for a while, telling her all about the room, how I'd washed down the woodwork with white spirit before giving it two coats of gloss, how I'd had to leave the windows open until the paint dried so that they didn't stick shut. I talked on, about the bird that landed on the window ledge and about the cat that came in from the neighbour's apartment. I kept talking, about anything, until the sound of cars passing in the rain at the other end of the line became waves on the beach. Finally I stopped talking, wondering if she was listening, how long the credit would last, but I couldn't let go of the telephone, or stop looking out at the rain and thinking of the endless sea.

Tiling a Bathroom

with Fyodor Dostoevsky

Tools:
Hammer
Spirit level
Scraper
Tile cutter
Sponge
Wooden batten
Tape measure
Dust sheet

Materials:
Tiles
Spacers
Tile adhesive
Tile grout

With a sort of stoic resignation Pokoroff rang the doorbell of the apartment on K—— Street. The threadbare bag of tools that he held in his hand now seemed to him pathetically inadequate for one claiming to be a fully served tiler and he hoped the old woman would not notice the deception. His ragged clothes, smeared and shiny with oil, were only to be expected on one about to undertake dirty work and now, down to his last few kopeks, the student was desperate for money. Behind the door, he could hear the old lady's slippered feet shuffling along the hall and, at the sound of a bolt being pulled aside, he tightened his grip on the rough handle and composed himself. Two eyes peered out at him from the interior. "Is that all you have brought?" said their owner distrustfully.

"I have what I need. Could you please show me to the bathroom?" As he spoke he fancied there was a gleam of mockery in the widow's eyes. A musty odour emerged from the old woman's lodgings and Pokoroff pushed past her with the air of one who tries to appear confident, but does so only with great pains.

The heat in the apartment was stifling as she led him through a small parlour. The light here seemed to be of a yellow or rather greenish hue, and Pokoroff's eye was drawn to the mantelpiece, where a collection of holy images competed for space with a group of rustic figures in porcelain, and a bitter smile played about our hero's lips. "Here we are batuchka. My son-in-law has left the materials there under the sink. I will be back around four."

Pokoroff's heart sank as he now contemplated the repulsive character of his surroundings. Above the basin a spotted mirror reflected an ancient tub, itself discoloured by the dirty brown stain that led from dripping tap to plughole. A rickety table, topped with jars of bath salts, separated the

"IS THAT ALL?"
HE EXCLAIMED

HE PLUNGED THE RUSTY
BLADE BEHIND THE TILES

BRANDISHING THE HATCHET,
HE SWUNG IT.

HE BEGAN LAYING ON
THE TILE ADHESIVE

HE TOOK A PAIL WHICH
HE FILLED WITH GROUTING
POWDER

POKOROVRUSHED FROM THE
BACK DOOR OF THE APARTMENT

bath from the newly disinfected toilet bowl, while between mirror and basin a cracked splashback, missing a brace of tiles, clung precariously to the wall. A sliver of soap and a chipped glass, containing a set of false teeth and a balding toothbrush, completed the inventory.

"Perhaps you could leave me a little money in advance," said our hero, pretending to take stock of the materials left by the son-in-law. In later times Pokoroff would wonder at his own cunning. "It is conceivable that I may need more adhesive or grouting before the day is done."

The old woman took a white leather pouch from her bag and undid its clasp. The greasy purse must have contained over a hundred roubles and, not wishing to arouse suspicion, Pokoroff diverted his gaze to the sinciput of the old lady's head where scant curls failed to conceal her pallid scalp in the greenish light. A sudden pressure in his hand brought him back to himself and with a scornful look he observed the ten-rouble note she had pressed into his palm.

"Is that all?" he exclaimed with excessive irritation.

Perceiving his disappointment the old lady smiled. "Well, let me pay you for your work now, and if you have cause to buy more materials I will refund the difference later." And so saying she counted fifty roubles into our hero's trembling hand. "I'm sure I can trust you to do a good job."

The self-styled tiler crammed the notes into the pocket of his ragged coat and, discerning an interrogatory note in this last statement, knitted his brows as he watched her leave the apartment, closing the door behind her.

For the first time, Pokoroff now opened the bag of tools he had stolen from the tool shed at the back of his lodgings and cast on its aged contents a look of flashing rage. "To think that I have been such a fool," he muttered. He saw now that the bag contained not the tools of his landlady, but those of her gardener. "This is exactly the sort of trifle that could spoil everything."

Feeling crushed, nay humiliated, he caught up the gardener's sickle and plunged its rusty blade behind the tiles above the sink. Long age and humidity had weakened the glue that held them in place so that they easily came away, crashing into the sink and shattering with a great noise as they did so. Their removal revealed an ugly rectangular patch of ridged and hardened adhesive. Pokoroff scraped now at this in an attempt to render the surface smooth, but the glue, so ineffective at holding the tiles in place, showed more resistance at clinging to the wall. Using a stabbing action the worker saw that little chips of the dried adhesive broke off, occasionally flying up into his face, and in this way he gradually succeeded in levelling the most irregular ridges formed by the glue.

The old woman, as is the way with old women who leave nothing to chance, had left a sack for rubbish and Pokoroff now began filling it with the debris from the sink. The jagged edges of the broken tiles were sharp and when he saw that a crack had appeared on the surface of the basin, he flew into a rage. How could he have been so unthinking? He might easily have placed some covering over the basin to cushion the fall of the tiles. With bitter disgust he saw that he had also managed to cut himself and that blood was dripping from his hand. It had already splashed his shoes and the floor before he thought to hold the wound over the open refuse bag. The thick red liquid dripped onto the broken tiles where the drops stained their white surface red. He grew light-headed and for a moment it seemed to him that the tiles were smiling at this benediction, until he realised that this was no chimera. Half buried in the detritus, the widow's false teeth came as a disagreeable surprise. In his haste he had forgotten to clear the room. "Details, details," he murmured and, looking up, he saw clearly the remains of the glass that had held the teeth mingling with the broken tiles in the sink. Reluctantly he recovered the gory teeth and dropped them out of sight into his pocket. He then wrapped his injured hand with a rag and watched as the white fabric turned red with blood.

Pokoroff felt giddy. Desperate to escape the stifling

Fyodor Dostoevsky

atmosphere of the apartment, he headed for the back door, which led to a small yard. He stood on the step, breathing deeply and offering up his face to the breeze. As he did so he beheld a line full of laundry, no doubt washed and hung out to dry that very morning while he himself had still been abed, struggling to rise after a night of disturbed and unrefreshing slumber.

He snatched a handkerchief from the line and replaced the bloody rag, which he hung up to dry in its place. Looking about him, he then tore a large sheet free from its pegs and returned to the bathroom, where he used it to protect the fading white enamel of the bathtub. Our worker was in a hurry to be gone and now he did not hesitate. Taking up the sickle he set about him, stabbing frantically at the walls, levering tiles loose in ones and twos, until the walls stood bare and the bath groaned under the weight of the debris.

Burning with impatience he tore open the package of tiles and with a piece of garden twine measured one of the sides. His plan was to attach a batten, procured expressly for the purpose, to the wall at precisely the height of the second row of tiles. This would prevent the tiles sliding down the wall, and ensure that they were level and did not follow the slope of the bath. He placed two of the masonry nails between his lips and took up the batten, but he was now interrupted in his work. Where was the hammer? Spitting out the nails, he

searched the bag again, turning it upside down and shaking
it until a garden trowel and a hatchet fell onto the bathroom
floor. A sickly smile appeared on his lips. Lacking a spirit
level, he did his best to confirm the batten was indeed level.
There was now not a moment to lose. Brandishing the
hatchet, he swung it, almost mechanically, on to the head of
the first nail. The sharp fixing penetrated the soft wood. With
increasing vigour Pokoroff struck two more blows, driving
the nail on into the wall. He checked again the level of the
batten, held up a second nail and, with his full strength,
drove the nail clear through wood and plaster, pinning the
piece of wood in place. It was done. Thick drops of sweat
trickled down his neck as he began laying on the tile
adhesive, a few feet at a time. His hands shaking, his lips
parched, he pressed each tile into place with a kind of
monomania. Among the materials left by his employer,
Pokoroff found a packet of tiny white plastic crosses and
these he used to ensure the tiles were evenly spaced. A desire
to escape these scornful lodgings made him desperate.
Without a tile cutter he used the garden shears to cut the last
pieces for the corners of the room before finally he turned to
renew the half-dozen tiles above the handbasin.

How many obstacles, how many tasks yet stood between
our hero and his freedom. The wooden batten was still
attached to the wall and the grouting required mixing before

it could be used to fill the grid of gaps that lay between the tiles. Bracing one foot in the bath, he pulled at the batten, he heaved, but the nail held fast. His impatience was intense as he used the hatchet to lever off the offending article. When finally it gave way, Pokoroff lurched backwards, the hatchet flew from his hand, crossed the narrow width of the room and landed with a crash in the basin. This time a deep jagged crack split the white cranium of the sink from tap to plughole. Pokoroff staggered back in disbelief, prey to sombre thoughts that his way of going to work was probably not the one circumstances demanded. Time was drawing on and the old lady might return at any moment.

From the kitchen he then took a pail, which he filled with grouting powder, adding sufficient water to make a smooth paste, before leaving the compound to stand. Pokoroff then applied the last of the adhesive to the wall where the batten had lately been removed, and fixed the final row of tiles in place. The grouting was now ready, but Pokoroff stood irresolute, until footsteps resounded on the landing. Scarcely daring to breathe, Pokoroff listened. When finally a key was pushed into the lock, the rattling of the handle shook him from his torpor. Pokoroff closed the bathroom door. Frantically he now began to slop grouting into the gaps; one by one the tiny white crosses between the tiles disappeared from sight beneath the grey paste. The mistress of the house could be heard calling aloud, "Batuchka! I am back. I will make some some tea. Will you take a cup?" The grouting done, he took up the damp sponge and began to wipe away the grey paste that splattered tiles, bath, clothing, everything. He was now in full possession of his intellect. Avoiding his reflection as he washed his hands, Pokoroff saw that the sink was shattered. From the cracked basin water spurted out in streams onto the floor. "Do not come in yet," he called aloud, "I have a surprise for you." He then took up the hatchet from the floor and, with a heave, hoisted the four corners of the sheet from the bath and made of it a sackful of broken tiles that he slung over his shoulder.

With a cry of "Close your eyes . . ." Pokoroff rushed out of the back door of the apartment. Stooping under his load, he passed under the red rag that hung from the line, staggered down the steps into the garden, and swung the sheet and its contents over the fence to land with a crash in the neighbouring yard. He then climbed up onto the garden wall and jumped down into the street.

On landing he fell awkwardly. A sharp pain coursed through his hip, but there was no time to stop. He limped on, trying to merge unseen with the afternoon crowds, to quit the neighbourhood before the widow had time to raise the alarm. He no longer felt shame at being seen in clothes stained by common labour, rather a fierce pride, the pride of one who earns his living by the sweat of his brow and the strength of his limbs, whose wounds are the honours of battle. Tired physically, he saw before him the promise of restful slumber, of the peace afforded to one whose work bears fruit for all, whose efforts bring dignity and salvation.

Suddenly he found himself the subject of catcalls; a drunk swaying on the steps of the dram house drew the attention of passers-by with a shout: "Look at the polka dancer!" He was now mimicking the wayward, loping gait of the injured Pokoroff. He tried to increase his speed, to outpace the tipsy clown, but the pain in his hip grew more acute. Pokoroff turned to confront his accuser. "What are you driving at? I am a worker. You would do well to take note that I have tiled a bathroom today with my own hands!" A busy public thoroughfare was no place to remedy matters and Pokoroff was obliged to stumble on, accompanied by the play-acting of the drunkard, his efforts to outpace him rendered more painful by the pressure of the old woman's false teeth as they bit deep into his thigh.

Putting up a Shelf

with Julius Caesar

Tools:
Drill
Screwdriver
Spirit level

Materials:
Wood for shelf
Brackets
Screws
Rawlplugs

The house comprised three areas, the upper floor, dominated by the Adulesceni, the ground floor, under the control of Caeasar's wife, and the external land, all under the sole control of Caesar himself. By granting autonomy to the rulers of these other areas Caesar hoped better to keep the peace, but recently Caesar's wife had petitioned him, arguing that her territory was too small. The ground floor was divided into lounge, dining room, study and kitchen, and it was in the area of the kitchen that Caesar's wife complained of insufficient space and work surfaces. Caesar was informed that a large part of the work space was taken up with condiments, appliances and recipe books, and he saw that there was a need for a shelf to relieve congestion.

Caesar's wife is in almost daily conflict with the Adulesceni, either trying to keep them out of her territory or raiding their settlements on the upper floor with the aim of imposing her customs and laws. The Adulesceni are known for their hostility and cruelty, even to their own kind; their territory on the upper floor consisted of two rooms, virtually closed to outsiders. The bathroom, designated as a neutral area open to all, had now also come under their domination.

As a tribe the Adulesceni are exempt from almost all work and do not pay taxes like ordinary citizens. They regard it as their greatest glory to lay waste as much as possible of the land around them so as to make it uninhabitable. The gods they reverence change almost constantly and they decorate their dwellings and clothing with images of the god most in favour. They also worship the Greek god Nike and the old Norse god Nokia, in his ever changing forms. They measure their time not by days but by nights and their belief that the day begins at night is supported by their sleeping for most of the daylight hours. They regard it as unbecoming to be seen in the presence of their parents and those who preserve their chastity least are most highly commended by their friends.

The customs of Caesar's wife are entirely different. The only gods she recognises are things that she can see and by which she is obviously benefited, such as the sun, jewels,

fabrics, slaves; the other gods she has never even heard of. Though she talks often of making sacrifices, she and her tribe are not much given to the practice. She is fiercely competitive with others of her kind and they make almost weekly raids on the merchants in search of plunder, which she often presents as a tribute to the Adulesceni. These raids are a constant nuisance to Caesar and the treasury.

For this reason Caesar recognised that he must act soon to remedy her complaints and immediately gave orders for the necessary materials to conduct the campaign. Caesar levied wood for a shelf measuring two metres long, twenty centimetres deep and two and a half centimetres thick, three brackets to be placed at regular intervals, screws and Rawlplugs. He also gathered tools – a drill with number eight masonry bit, a screwdriver and a spirit level.

Caesar chose to locate the shelf directly above the work surface but within reach of Caesar's wife. Above the worktop was situated a light switch. Caesar had been informed that concealed wiring extended above this switch in a direct line vertically. Caesar wanted to avoid locating the brackets along this axis and positioned the shelf accordingly.

But before his arrangements were completed a deputation arrived from the Adulesceni to complain that the curfew set in the district kept them from proper worship of their gods and was causing them to lose face before other members of their tribe. In addition there was to be a gathering of their people which, if they were unable to attend, would damage their standing immeasurably.

When Caesar reminded them of their responsibilities to their mother, who had extended her protection, and in calling them children recalled their failure to observe the rules of the home by the recent smuggling of banned substances into Caesar's own quarters, they prostrated themselves before him with tears in their eyes. Caesar reminded them of the important privileges conferred upon them by himself and by his wife. Caesar answered the deputation that he would consider the matter, but now insisted that they leave with him a hostage who would serve in the current undertaking. The deputation, on hearing of Caesar's request, hung their heads in dejection, their eyes fixed upon the ground, such is the Adulesceni's hatred of work. In astonishment Caesar reminded them of the consequences if they failed to pay tribute to him, so Caesar prevailed.

Thus, while the hostage held the shelf in position Caesar took the spirit level and, placing it on the wooden surface, made adjustment so that the shelf was horizontal. Fearing that the hostage could not be trusted to hold the length of wood steady for long, Caesar drew a line in pencil under the shelf. Caesar then took the first bracket and positioned it towards one end of the line, taking care to keep the bracket

both vertical and level with the underside of the shelf. Caesar
then marked the three holes of the bracket on the wall and
took up his drill with the number eight masonry bit. He
drilled the first hole and filled it with a Rawlplug. When
Caesar saw that the hole was so deep that the Rawlplug was
now out of reach of the screw, he wrapped a piece of tape
round the drill bit, one Rawlplug's length from its point.
The next two holes went according to plan and Caesar was
able to screw the first bracket into place.

Now when he saw Caesar's full attention on the task in
hand, the hostage broke ranks and made his escape. Know
that all men naturally love freedom and hate servitude; the
Adulesceni moreover are fond of idleness and angry to be
brought from their settlements in daylight. Engaged as he
was in operations on the east wall, Caesar was unable to fight
on two fronts and could not put down the rebellion straight
away. Caesar decided to allow the hostage to leave, but not to
let the rebellion go unpunished in case the Adulesceni
should despise him for weakness.

The drilling for the second bracket showed the wall in
this section to be of plasterboard and not of brick. When the
first Rawlplug was lost in the action, falling into the cavity
behind the wall, Caesar saw that his labour was being wasted.
One device that Caesar had procured proved useful, special
Rawlplugs made for plasterboard. These were more conical

in shape and, when tightened with a screw, opened to better grip the plasterboard. With their aid the work was now a common task to which Caesar easily proved superior. The brackets fixed, Caesar put the shelf in place. One hour after collection of the timber had begun the work was completed. On the conclusion of the shelving campaign Caesar's wife came to offer congratulations with promises of peace and friendship, which Caesar graciously accepted. Caesar quartered his tools and marched on the Adulesceni stronghold where a grim struggle was anticipated. The speed of his advance, however, threw them into a sudden panic and Caesar, spurred on by the recollection of their earlier treachery, burst into their camp and, in a demonstration of strength, seized their god Ipod.

Caesar had achieved all the objects for which he had laboured, to overawe Caesar's wife, punish the Adulesceni and to relieve the kitchen of pressure on space. In this short period Caesar considered he had done all that honour or interest required.

Repairing a Dripping Tap

with Marguerite Duras

Tools:
Spanner

Materials:
Washer

The man passes for a second time in front of the house and stops. He rings the doorbell. The door is open, he enters. The interior is light, furnished in white. A woman's voice:

"So you've come."

She is standing. She watches. She watches a sink, a tap. He advances towards her. She sees him come. His clothes are dark. His eyes bright. She smiles. He takes one more step, he stops beside her. With a mechanical gesture she shows the tap. From the tap, drips of water fall into the sink. The tap is watched.

The light fades.

Man, woman, tap. He moves, he opens the tap. The noise of water growing louder, the falling water thunders, shattering white in the sink to disappear into the abyss, to join other tributaries, and channels forming a great mass of water, going down to the sea. To the caverns of the sea. He closes the tap. The noise subsides. Silence. The silence is broken by the dripping of the tap.

"I think the washer's gone."

She speaks. Her tone requires no reply.

"The washer's gone."

He replies.
Drips fall one by one. Drops of water that refuse to wait in the darkness of the pipe for permission to run.

"He does it up too tight. He doesn't like the tap to drip," she says.

The man bends to turn off the water supply. Then he straightens, he opens the tap fully. Briefly the noise of running water returns. Suddenly the water stops. The dripping stops. Silence. Outside, beyond the terrace, dusk descends on the town. The light runs out of the sky, draining into the west. Now, in the silence, the sound of the sea reaches into the kitchen. The sea, formless, uncontained, untapped, beyond compare. A scream cries out, like the sound of a woman falling.

*

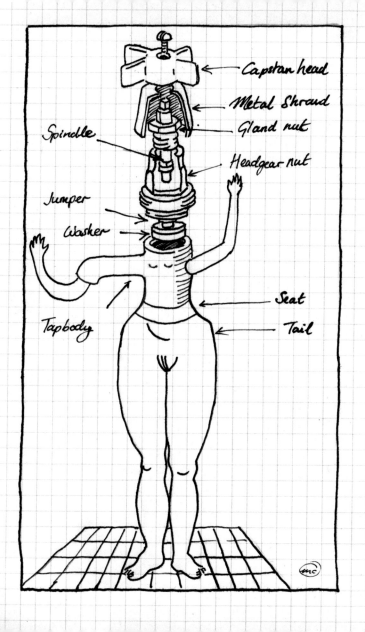

Capstan head

Metal Shroud

Gland nut

Spindle

Headgear nut

Jumper

Washer

Tapbody

Seat

Tail

"What was that?" he asks

"What?" She lifts her face slightly. He is not looking at her.

"That cry."

"Nothing. The sound of the gulls."

The story begins.

Between the man and the window the woman is walking; her hand raised like a child's, she covers her eyes. The floorboards creak beneath her feet. In front of him the tap. He rests his hand on the shiny metal. He sees the capstan head, beneath the head the shroud covers the gland nut, the spindle, the headgear nut, the jumper. Beneath the jumper, out of sight, the flattened washer, compressed, decomposed, destroyed.

The man unscrews the metal shroud to reveal a large nut just above the body of the tap. With a spanner he unfastens the nut, he removes the headgear of the tap. He detaches the streaming mechanism, he offers it to her. The light dances in his eyes.

"The washer's gone."

They look, they look at each other, they wait.

He repeats,

"The washer's gone. Look, look here, look."

He shows her the washer, laid waste, the ravages of time, the build-up of limescale, the pressure created by the ever tightening tap, fighting to hold back the flow, the tide. The brutal accumulation of force.

She says she understands. She makes an effort not to cry.

With a screwdriver he prises off the old washer, cracked, wrinkled, prematurely aged. He takes a new one from his toolbox. The new washer sits pertly in his hand, smooth, firm, thick as cream on milk. It slips tightly over the little button on the jumper at the base of the headgear. He replaces the mechanism into the tap, screwing it tightly back into place, he lowers the shroud, the shiny cover that hides the tap's mechanism beneath a coat of gleaming metal, he bends down, he opens the mains valve. The last of the light drains from the sky, in the darkness they hear the water forced back into the pipe, hear the pressure rise beneath the washer. He straightens, opens the tap, he closes the tap. They watch. They wait. Nothing drips. Nothing flows. Everything is stopped, everything is held back.

He returns his spanner to the toolbox. He looks at her.

"You're crying."
"I'm crying?"

Silence.

She is standing next to him, but her eyes look into the distance, at the last fiery clouds as they slip one by one over the horizon.

Boarding an Attic

with Edgar Allan Poe

Tools:
Claw hammer
Ripsaw

Materials:
Floor-grade chipboard
Nails
Wood adhesive

The long and weird catalogue of human misery has its own dark hierarchy. Accounts of flood and famine, plague and pestilence, earthquake and eruption rightfully thrill us and command the attention of our most august journals, the sympathy of our governments and the generosity of our charitable societies. Yet can the misery of the individual who shares his fate with friend and neighbour, citizen and countryman, neath the ineluctable and unforeseeable wrath of whatever Authority he chooses to honour, bear comparison with the true wretchedness and ultimate woe of one who suffers in the knowledge that he alone has cultivated the seeds of his own destruction? The good husband, who sought to surprise his spouse with a new electrical light fitting, awaited her return in smouldering convulsions, his deadly caress an extension of the galvanic wire. The Sunday arborist who fell from his ladder, still clutching the hired chainsaw, no more merciful than Death's scythe, to harvest the soul of his wife, deadheading roses below him. Such handymen have truly walked the shores of the Ultima Thule of torment.

Over long years I had amassed a vast collection of papers relating to these and other such incidents. Books, journals, newspaper cuttings, actuarial reports and more, all gathered in the course of my profession, accumulated in my study and beyond, until there was scarce space to admit the rare visitor who still troubled to call on me. Eventually that rare caller, my friend and physician, Doctor Garrett, prevailed upon me to create a separate storehouse for my collection and so liberate the living quarters of my residence from a burden that threatened to engulf them completely. So did I find myself in the cathedral-like structure of commingled gloom and grandeur that occupied the uncharted peaks of the ancient and dilapidated property wherein I had made my home. My intention was to lay a floor. To this end I had made measurements and caused to be delivered a quantity of floor-grade chipboard of the tongue-and-groove variety. Working from the corner furthest from the feeble light source, which scarce illumined my labours, I began to lay the boards. Those dark recesses, unlooked upon since that cloak of slate first enveloped them in eternal night, resisted my intrusion like

the densest thicket. Lost in a forest of strut and rafter, hangar and purlin, my feet stumbled through the rootlike joists and my every fibre thrilled with the hostility of those timber brakes.

The first of the boards I laid at right angles to the joist. I then drove two-inch nails through the heavy sheet, down into balk and beam, the joist and noggin that comprised the supporting structure. Restricted in the free movement of my limbs in those cramped conditions, the first strike of the hammer fell false, the nail bent and, discovering the instrument of their burial to be without claw, I was unable to extract the nail from the board whose vicelike grip now held it fast and so I beat the nail down, flattening its deformity into the floor-grade chipboard until it could scarce be seen.

So I continued, staggering the boards like brickwork, single-minded in my desire to produce a work that would astound the doctor with its thoroughness. I glued each joint generously and, using a block of wood between the hammer and the sheet material, so as not to damage the tongue, I beat the next board close so that the glue oozed and bubbled from the sutures as blood from a wound. With a damp cloth I wiped away this excess before it could scab and dry.

Time and again the hammer swung, driven by my own

locomotion, tracing its relentless arc, striking at times on steel, at others on wood, sending the metal fixings vibrating deep into the board. In time I noted that five or six such vibrations or blows would bring the head of each nail level with the surface of the chipboard and by dint of my toil the boards increased their dominion over the wooden framework, to sink finally like fangs biting one by one to close and lock their prey in a deathly grip.

How many hours I crawled on my knees about that low timber framework I could not say. At times some breath or vapour threatened to extinguish the flickering light and in those moments I feared to step blindly into the void, to crash through the fragile plasterwork, that lay like a trap all about me, falling to I know not what fate and to what additional labours.

At others, hearing the echoes of my blows resound in that dark vault, I desisted from my labours, imagining a sound or presence there behind me in the shadows. Sometimes I remained perfectly still, listening in the gloom, nor saw I aught, but the malignant echo continued my companion, its metallic and clangorous reverberation, muffled as though at great distance, unerring as it beat a counterpoint that made itself felt in the hairs on the back of my neck.

The day wore on and with each passing hour the expanse of chipboard spread about me like the incoming tide. Soon I found I could walk freely in those areas new boarded. My hands and knees rejoiced in their newfound freedom, and I felt the blood return to my tired limbs. I lost all sense of time, but feeling the air grow cold I knew that night had fallen over the vacant fields of rank sedge that surrounded the lonely old house. I now thrilled to think of the space I had created in that antre, vast and idle, wherein my precious collection would take its place. I judged each board sufficient in length and breadth to hold a year's collection; soon there would be space enough to hold the records of a lifetime, the catalogue of death and folly that I kept as a warning to my fellow actuaries.

In time the smell of glue and treated wood, oppressive to my respiration, hung thick in the still air, but on I toiled, limbs aching, palms and fingers tender from long handling of the boards, their rough edges so unlike the smooth files and documents that comprised the responsibilities of my professional life. I proceeded here with the same diligence of action, with the same obsessive energy that so characterised my research – I resolved to leave not one square foot fallow in the large and lofty chamber. My tired eyes, however, fought now to reach the remoter angles of the chamber, the recesses where I struggled to fit the last pieces of the puzzle. As my labours drew to their diabolic conclusion I pulled the lantern close to the area in which I now fitted the final boards. Its sulphurous lustre cast long shadows on the angled surfaces about me and I saw the black shadow of the hammer held in my fist aloft, yet whether through inanition or some strange flickering of the flame the shadow appeared to begin its descent before its parent.

Making haste to keep pace, my own blow missed its mark and I recoiled in pain. As I clutched at the engorged extremity my involuntary motion caused the lantern to fall, spilling fuel and flame onto the fresh dry wood, made more flammable by the gaseous fumes of the adhesive. The flame caught; in moments I would have been engulfed, had I hesitated to smother the conflagration with my own hands and body. The smell of burnt hair and flesh filled my nostrils, but my swift reaction had extinguished the fire. I rolled back, my eyes trying in vain to pierce that ebon darkness, and cradling my injured hands I struggled towards the hatch that led below to the comfort of my living quarters. No feeble gleam relieved the profundity of that primeval gloom and my blistered fingers now began to feel their way across the new flooring, tracing each seam and joint towards the centre of that domelike cavern. The miasmatic vapours that rose from the drying glue lay like a mist on my blind path and the incubus of alarm settled on my soul. As I continued my course, my fingers probing ahead into the gloom like the antennae of some great insect, my sense of dread accelerated until a long low groan involuntarily escaped from my lungs. For you, reader, to conceive of the horror of my sensations is, I presume, utterly impossible. Time after time I extended my arm, hoping and praying to feel the void beneath me, the open hatch that would free me from this infernal chamber, so that now I would have rejoiced to find myself falling headlong to injury and freedom, even death. But at every turn my blind probing fell upon the resistance of well-fitted, floor-grade chipboard, made fast by my own labours.

Long days have passed since I laid the deck of the unbreachable hold in which I make my final voyage. Cargo-like I sprawl, my leg, most unnatural in its configuration, broken in the fall from the roofbeam. In the darkness I lie twice blinded; my senseless fingers, torn and bleeding from long hours spent scratching and tearing at joint and nail, my eyes redundant in the darkness. My strength, following that long departed cherub, Hope, is gone. My nerves have been unstrung.

I am woken from sleep, no! from swoon, from delirium. A single beam of light falls on my sunken countenance. Ha ha, through the slateless crevice, made before my fall, I see his eye peering down. I hear the flapping of his dark wings, the scratching of his clawlike toes. My parched lips, bitter from sucking at the damp and glue-soaked cloth, writhe in welcome with a senseless locution.

The hateful eye watches me now almost constantly. I see him. And I hear his kindred, gathering on the rooftop. An unkindness of ravens, waiting, waiting to gather me up, parcel by parcel. I can write no more. Dear Doctor, ensure this record finds its way into my collection. Then set a match to them all.

The Great Red Porcupine Trapped in the Snake Pit Narco Guerrilla Gardening

OR

Putting Up a Garden Fence

with Hunter S. Thompson

Tools:
Spade or post auger
Spirit level
Hammer
Saw

Materials:
Fence posts
Arris rails
Featheredge boards
Post mix or sand cement and hardcore
Nails
Brackets

To my mind the corvette convertible is the only vehicle that can carry a ten-foot length of timber in style, but when it comes to making a handbrake turn or high-speed manoeuvres in excess of a hundred miles per hour, it begins to show its limitations as a serious hauler of lumber. By the time we arrived back at the house the car looked like it had been involved in a high-speed collision with Uncle Tom's Cabin. As I lowered the volume on Dylan's "Subterranean Homesick Blues" and extricated myself from the woodpile I could hear the voice of my attorney somewhere in the thicket of timbers that had sprouted in the seat next to me: "Man, this is no way to travel." What remained of the ten ten-foot arris rails, five ten-foot gravel boards, eighty four-foot featheredge boards and six eight-foot four-inch by four-inch sawn posts we'd stacked so neatly in the bucket seat was now piled against the windshield. In the trunk six bags of post mix (a lethal concoction of ready-mixed hardcore, sand and cement), twenty brackets and six pounds of nails made the car's nose point skyward so that it looked like a giant red porcupine was trying to climb up onto the sidewalk. It was important to keep my attorney's spirits up while I assessed his chances of survival. "Sweet Jesus, don't you just love the smell of fresh-cut timber in the morning?" I asked. "Can you move your legs?"

"Fuck no. I'm paralysed, call a doctor, a real doctor. Those

bastards from the Pentagon have been testing some kind of napalm down at Bob's Premier Sheds and Fencing. My leg won't bend." Sure enough the Samoan's leg was rigid as I pulled it out across the passenger seat. Something was protruding from just above the knee and I feared that, in the emergency stop, he had suffered an open fracture. In his current state I doubted he was capable, but as a doctor I had to ask, "Are you in pain?"

"I can't feel a fucking thing."

"That's good." He needed to be reassured. "The bone has probably cut straight through the nerve." His screaming was cut short when he saw the neighbour peering from the window. "What's that old bitch looking at?" Now that he'd stopped screaming I felt emboldened to investigate the wound. "Hold still," I said, sliding the blade of an eight-inch hunting knife up his trouser leg and opening the fabric to the knee.

"How does it look?" he asked, still looking up at the house.

"You'll walk again." I put on my best $800 a day (TV not inclusive) bedside manner and removed the four-foot featheredge board that had somehow inserted itself in the great Samoan's trouser leg. "The pants, however, might not make it."

"This is my best fucking suit. Who's going to employ me

like this? ARE YOU HAPPY NOW?" This last comment was screamed at the window of the clapboard villa where my neighbours were no doubt already calling the police.

When he'd recovered the feeling in his legs we unloaded the materials onto the lawn. I drove a wooden peg into the ground at each end of the fence run and stretched a line between. I then marked the position of the fence posts, avoiding tree roots and landmines. I instructed my attorney to start digging and waited for the mescaline to kick in.

As the Samoan slammed his spade into the ground he stopped to look back over his shoulder. "There's someone watching us," he said.

"It'll be the neighbour," I said. "It's a small town."

"As your attorney, I advise you to kill her. Once she's seen where we bury this stuff, what's to stop her coming over to dig it up after dark?"

The guy at the timber yard had told us if we buried one quarter of the post the rest should stand up well in a hurricane. "Don't worry," I said. "With six feet of post sticking out of the ground to mark where we buried the other two, I don't think this is a secret we can keep for long. Just keep digging, we don't want to look suspicious."

He lifted a size-eleven foot onto the spade, his leg peeking coquettishly through the slit trouser leg, and the blade sank into the ground. There was a lot to do. As project leader my immediate task was to recover the quart of Wild Turkey we had left on the back seat of the car.

At some point after removing the top from the bottle I must have passed out. When I came round I could hear the dry thud of spade on earth and the rattle of pebbles against steel. My attorney was still digging. I looked out into the garden but he was nowhere to be seen. Holy shit, I thought, the sound of digging has burnt itself onto the retina of my ear. I'm cursed to hear it for ever, like the rhythm section of . . . Then I saw a flurry of dust fly up from the ground and the sound stopped.

"Help. Somebody fucking get me out of here!"

Either the mescaline had worn off or my attorney had reached a tricky point of law. I staggered out into the garden; as I reached the site of the first post, the empty bottle fell from my hand. The hole was now about seven feet deep and the eminent Samoan, still in his business suit, was thrashing at the ground and dancing, like his feet were on fire. "Snakes, they're coming up through the ground. As soon as I cut the head off one, another one appears. Get me out of here!"

Somehow I pulled him from the hole and the two of us lay panting for breath on the ground. "Don't worry," I said, "if it's long enough, we can beat them to death with the fence post."

To reassure the great excavator that the snakes would not

be climbing out of the hole, and to add some much needed drainage, I threw the contents of a bucket of hardcore, mostly broken bricks and small stones, down into the depths, shouting, "Eat hardcore, you scaly motherfuckers."

By the time I looked up the Samoan was standing over me, stripped to the waist holding a shotgun. I had a perfect view of the inside of both barrels. "You filthy bastard," he said. "How long have you known about those snakes? I oughta blow your fucking head off." I was on my knees over a vertical grave deep enough to bury a man upright, two men even, if packed carefully, with a drug-crazed attorney in slit pants aiming a shotgun at my head. There were signs that I might be losing control of the situation.

"You're fired," I said.

"What do you mean, I'm fired?"

"As a qualified doctor I can see that you've not been taking your medication. I can't afford to carry sick men on this job."

"Oh, Jesus," he groaned, relaxing the gun into the crook of his arm, "I forgot." From his pocket the Samoan produced a salt cellar of cocaine and poured a line onto the back of his hand. When he'd finished walking his nose along the line he licked off the residue, sucked his teeth and said, "As your attorney, I advise you to mark the position of the next hole and stand aside."

Putting Up a Garden Fence

The spade was lying in the bottom of the snake pit but the Samoan knew that the refusal to give up is at the heart of the American Dream. He set his feet wide apart over the mark and, at close range, fired the shotgun straight down into the ground. There was no doubting his reasoning, a hole seemed the logical consequence. While I set out the blue floral sunloungers and mixed two more tequilas, he let off the second barrel and reloaded. Lying there I gazed dreamily up at the sunlight twinkling through the leaves. My eyelids hung heavy behind gold-rimmed shades as I sipped on my sunrise, listening to the explosive bass line of the Samoan's dirt shoot. Somewhere between cartridge twenty and fifty the tequila began to cut through the drugs. Fine luck it would be if the police now arrived at the door.

"You say you're a doctor? Well, now, doctor, you more than anyone should be aware that a twelve-bore shotgun is not a suitable tool to be used when erecting a fence."

"I'm sorry, officer, but this was an urgent case. The neighbour's dog has been pissing on my marijuana, I mean my dahlia collection. We worked its owner over so badly with the spade that now it doesn't dig straight. Perhaps you could lend a hand."

What happened next convinced me that somehow, in between the wood yard and the house, probably when we swerved at high speed to avoid the crazy guy in the wheelchair on the sidewalk, we had entered, like Connecticut Yankees, some weird kind of Twain's World.

Someone was ringing the doorbell, they were desperate to see us and weren't going away. Through the side light in the hall I could see a patrol car parked behind the porcupine. "It's the cops," I said.

The Samoan offered me the shotgun. "As your attorney, I advise you not to be taken alive." He was still twisted, but I persuaded him to drop the weapon into the snake hole and remove the salt cellar from his left nostril.

When faced with a house call from the police never greet them politely – this will only arouse suspicion in the cop gut. The thing to do is to launch immediately into the role of the indignant citizen and demand an explanation. "What the hell kept you, officer? I could have been killed, he must have fired off sixty rounds before we chased him into the shrubbery. He could still be hiding in the potting shed."

I opened the door to face my accusers; two patrolmen were brandishing a stack of four-foot featheredge board. Holy shit, Bob's Premier Sheds and Fencing is supplying the police department too. My brain locked up, but my mouth was already loose. "He's still in the garden, officer, I think he'll come quietly now." It looked like I'd have to get my hands dirty on this one and my chief excavator was about to be buried.

The cop laughed. "Seriously, sir, a load should be properly fastened before you go on the highway. We followed the trail of timber to the wood store where they gave us your address and a description of your vehicle. A convertible is not suitable for the transportation of large loads of timber. Would you mind letting us in, this stuff's getting heavy."

I thought I was hallucinating. For the first time in my life I'd found a cop who was trying to protect and serve, home delivery included. The great magnet was pulling in my direction and it felt good.

"So what brings you guys to the neighbourhood? You're new around here, right?" They dropped the boards onto the lawn and then saw my attorney. He was crouched over the pit, his head moving from side to side in a snakelike motion.

"Wow, that's a hell of a foundation you've dug there."

The Samoan was back on his feet. "Doctor, let me take care of this. Tell room service we'll need coffee." He took the patrolmen by the arm and began speaking in a whisper. "The good doctor here is a key part in the war on drugs and terror. In order to help combat the nationwide threat to the American way of life, he needs total quiet."

"No shit. You hear that, Ed? The doc's a big shot. Why is he here? We don't really have much of a problem with that stuff in Oatville."

"Oh, it's coming." I handed round coffee and offered the patrolmen some doughnuts that I'd found in the kitchen. The Samoan took a handful and began filling his pockets. "He hasn't had breakfast," I said apologetically.

The Samoan then snatched the last doughnut from my hand and continued his exposé: "Don't you guys read the papers? A hard rain's gonna fall and it's heading this way. If the doctor here doesn't succeed, your kids could all be dope fiends within a year. Why do you think we're fixing this fence? Here, hold this." While one of the cops held the post in a hole full of shot, my attorney used the spirit level to check it was straight. "Your people need to wake up or gangs of twisted junkies are going to be moving in all over the county. Officers, can I trust you?" Their mouths still full with doughnut, the two men nodded. The Samoan gave instructions to Officer Squane to pour one of the bags of cement mix in around the base of the four-inch by four-inch post and add a bucket of water. I mixed another round of tequilas and cleared the cups. I had yet to lay my hands on anything heavier than a cocktail stick and intended to keep it that way. I have no objection to heavy work, but I couldn't interfere with the workings of the great magnet.

The team kept working until all the posts were in the ground. As the cement was drying my attorney filled in the details of the plot against America.

"The producers can't grow their evil harvest on open farmland, that would be playing into the hands of the feds, and the crop-dusting air service, so they're growing the stuff in the homes of innocent Americans. Oh, yeah, Miss Maudie doesn't recognise that plant growing in her azaleas? You're sure as hell right she don't! She's part of the problem. That grade A narcotic harvest is growing in the gardens of America."

"Can you believe this stuff, Ed? What the hell's happening to this country?" I watched them listening to the Samoan's impassioned plea.

"It's not just the neighbour's dog walking through the hole in that fence. We're talking about a gateway to oblivion, a portal through which a million short-circuited, fucked-up, smack-headed freak kings are gonna be walking out onto the streets of this proud land. The stuff's not being smuggled over the border; it's not coming up the Hudson in a submarine; they're picking it straight from Miss Maudie's azalea patch. And no one's even watching. While we're watching the borders, these guerrilla narco gardeners are taking over the ground under our feet."

Patrolman Ed was strangely afflicted and starting to get jumpy. He had already begun cutting the rails to fit between the posts and it wasn't long before his okie partner was using the brackets to help the Samoan nail them into place.

"Hot damn, Ed! We better warn Old Man Mitchell. His fence is still down from that storm last September."

The police did everything they could to assist my attorney. The rails were now all in place and as the gravel boards were nailed to wooden cleats at the bottom of each post, the sound of hammering followed me into the kitchen. My legal team then began hammering the boards to the rails, until a call on the radio meant that we were left to finish off the last few without the protection of our local boys in blue. The hard work seemed to have taken its toll, they both looked kind of rubbery as they headed for their patrol car. The younger of the two, Ed, fell over as he tried to draw his handgun when a large shrub on the front lawn blocked his path. "Officer," I said to his partner, "this is all still highly confidential, we can't have the press getting hold of this story. I'd appreciate it if you didn't talk about this meeting." Their car lurched into reverse before driving off, weaving from side to side. I was laughing crazily as I stepped back into the house. "I think we should put them on the payroll," I said to my attorney.

"They could be looking for a job by the morning."

"What do you mean?"

"Those doughnuts you handed out."

"Yeah, what about them?"

"I wasn't expecting visitors, they were meant to be for us." I began to fear the worst. "I injected them with mescaline."

"You did what? A mescaline jam mix, that's a lethal concoction. I wouldn't want to be in Old Man Mitchell's shoes once that stuff kicks in. What are we going to do?"

"As your attorney I advise you to take this." From his pocket he then handed me a doughnut. I felt the jam running down my chin and a wave of happiness engulfed me as the mournful wail of a police siren drifted in over the fence on the evening breeze.

Applying Sealant Round a Bath

with Johann Wolfgang von Goethe

Tools:
Mastic gun
Small wedge-shaped piece of wood

Materials:
Silicone sealant
Washing-up liquid

22 May

Oh, my dear friend. What a thing our human destiny is! How happy I am to be embarking on a life in the country at last! Though I cannot say that I have yet met with any society, the solitude here is a balm, and I have already made all manner of acquaintance. A local handyman has become attached to me and will not have cause to regret it. Yesterday I sketched him replacing the guttering on a neighbour's house. I liked his way so spoke to him and asked after his circumstances. Presently we were acquainted and soon, as generally happens to me with this kind of person, intimate. What a serenity has taken possession of my soul since I arrived here in these paradisic parts.

Today he paid me a visit and was kind enough to

suggest a large number of improvements to the property, all of which, he assures me, he is more than able to assist with.

25 May

Thank you, my friend, for your warning. Though I well know he can never be my equal, my workman appears an honest type with most pleasing features and attitude. I shall scarcely be able to tell you with what enthusiasm he began work on the house. He is an open man of good heart and I see no reason to keep my distance for the sake of form.

On his suggestion I have paid him in advance and provided him with a set of keys. While I was away riding he removed that old iron bathtub, preparatory to replacing it with a magnificent modern bath and shower unit of such harmonious shape and proportion that my very soul is afire, longing and languishing to try it.

On my return, soaked and dirty from one of those early summer showers that strike with so little notice, the water supply was cut off, but the worthy fellow showed such grace and generosity in sharing with me the contents of his flask of coffee that I was reminded of that magnificent passage in Homer where Odysseus enjoys the hospitality of the excellent swineherd. What fools men are not to see the obstacles that class and privilege place before us.

29 May

How these beautiful spring mornings fill the heart. Today finally the young fellow returned. I cannot express the feelings that overwhelmed me as he busied himself installing the bathtub I described to you in my last letter. Indeed, I should need the gifts of the greatest poets if I were to recount his expressive gestures, the harmony and economy of his movement and the secret fire that shone in his eyes as he set about laying the copper pipes, shaping them to fit so neatly the contours of the room and using his blow torch to such brilliant effect.

The sight delighted me and I sat down on the toilet seat across from him and took great pleasure in drawing this domestic idyll. I added the tiles that formed a backdrop to his work, a towel and the sink, all simply the way it was. And I must congratulate myself on creating a harmonious study. Surely there is more of dignity and honour in one hour of manual labour than in a month of observing protocol and ceremony in the service of the ambassador.

6 June

I no longer know where I got to in my story. It has been more than a week now since I last saw my artisan. A few of his tools still lie abandoned on the bathroom floor, some small wooden wedges, a simple mastic gun and a tube of white silicone sealant. A jar, containing a solution of washing-up liquid, sits still on the window ledge. How their presence haunts me.

I supposed at first that he had perhaps taken ill, until today, when I caught sight of his van in front of another house in the vicinity. I waited for some time to speak with him. When finally, giving up hope, I left a note and walked on, a shout of laughter could be heard from the window. I could tear my heart open and beat my poor head on seeing how little people can mean to each other.

I grind my teeth; the devil take him! Ah, I have snatched up the gun a hundred times thinking to relieve my sorely beset heart.

11 June

Ah this void, this terrible void I feel in my breast. Still no reply or sign of progress. God knows how often I have regretted ever beginning this course of action. Woe! As ever, I fear you are right my friend. Toil and labour, joys and rewards, they cannot be separated.

14 June

The decision is taken. A thousand possibilities and plans raged in my heart but in the end it was there, one last fixed and definite thought. The gun is now in my hand and I am resolved to do whatever is necessary.

Applying Sealant Round a Bath

15 June

I placed the tube of sealant snugly in the mastic gun and, using only a simple pair of scissors, removed the extremity from the tube's tapered nozzle, so that, when squeezed, the amalgam, as white as the driven snow, was greater in girth than the gap between bath and tiles. What I told you recently concerning painting I can confirm is also true of applying bath sealant; what counts is that one conceives of a line of perfect breadth and straightness, and then dares to give it expression. Applying the steadiest of pressure to the trigger, I began, at one end of the bath, to lay down a steady flow of the sealant, and so to fill the abyss that had tortured me for so long. Then, from among the little wooden wedges I chose one, the width of my little fingernail, and put it to soak in the jar containing the washing-up solution before drawing it with a smooth and steady motion along the little ribbon of white that now joined bath and wall as one. I swear that every man should pass a few moments of each day in such common labour. Its simple pleasure is a balm to the heart.

Farewell. This letter will be to your taste, it is full of practical steps.

That evening I lay soaking in my tub. Through the window, above the chestnut trees illuminated in the moonlight, shone the stars that make up the blade of the Plough, my favourite and the most practical of all the heavenly bodies. But of all this I was hardly sensible. What overwhelmed me with emotion and made the world about me a very paradise, was the blue-white gleam of the sealant in the moonlight, its edges so straight, its surface a smooth and perfect barrier betwixt tile and tub, holding back the splashing foam that burst from the banks of the bath. In such moments the humblest labourer, fatigued by his exertions, surely floats more buoyantly on the waters of the measureless sea, soaks more deeply in the foaming pool of the Eternal and approaches more closely the blessed serenity of Him who makes all things.

Remedying a Drawer that Sticks

with Samuel Beckett

Materials:
Wax candle

ACT ONE

Two figures on a country road. Grey light fading to darkness. Between them, atop a small mound, sits a chest of drawers. The figure on the left, CONNOR, wears dark glasses; he is blind and carries a stick. On the right, GODARD. Both are looking at the piece of furniture.

GODARD. What are you waiting for? You won't find better. It's a lovely piece of work.
CONNOR. (*Stroking his hand along the surface of the chest and cocking his ear forward to listen*) Yes. Yes it is.
GODARD. It was made by my father you know.
CONNOR. Really. I never knew. (*Running his hands over the front of the cabinet.*) It could be just what I need.
GODARD. Believe me, a lovely piece of work.
CONNOR. Did it take him long?
GODARD. About a week I think, he made a lot of things.
CONNOR. It could do the job nicely. (*Feeling his way, he starts*

to walk round to the other side of the chest. As he walks
GODARD places his hands on the chest and turns it, moving
round so that though the two men exchange places, the front
is always facing CONNOR. The back of the chest is covered
with hardboard and has a hole. CONNOR looks up
momentarily from the chest towards GODARD.) How much
did you say you were looking for?

GODARD. You can't put a value on something like this, it
has sentimental connotations. A man's work you know. I
want it to go to a good home, somewhere that it will be
cherished.

CONNOR. Yes, yes, of course. A man's work. Would you
mind? . . . (CONNOR gestures with his hand to the front of
the drawer.)

GODARD. Not at all. Not at all, please. (He steps forward,
reaching for CONNOR's arm to help.)

CONNOR. (Pushing him off angrily) Don't you touch me. I can
do it.
(There is no handle on the drawer. For a while CONNOR
searches for the handle, then tries to grip the drawer by its
edges. Bent low, his head resting against the chest of drawers,
he listens, his fingers moving slowly around the joints in the
wood. Finally his face looks up in appeal. For a moment
GODARD looks at him blankly, then looks more closely at
CONNOR's dark glasses, then starts into action. He searches

through his pockets, pulls forth a screwed-up handkerchief and unwraps it to reveal a brass knob, which he then screws to a thread that protrudes at the front on the drawer. Delicately he places CONNOR's hands on the handle.)

GODARD. There you go.

CONNOR. That's more like it. (*He rubs his hands together, then pulls on the handle without success. Surprised.*) What have you got in here? (*Breathing heavily, he tries again, this time spitting on his hands before rubbing them together. He rattles the handle and tries once more.*) It won't budge.

GODARD. (*Irritated*) You're not pulling it straight. Get out the way. (*He pushes CONNOR to one side, then pulls on the handle, increasing his effort but without success.*) Well, lend a hand.

(*CONNOR holds GODARD round the waist and the two men pull. After much heaving and shouting the drawer opens about two inches.*)

GODARD. There. What did I say? You just have to pull it straight.

CONNOR. (*Feeling the opening with his fingers*) It's not exactly open, is it.

GODARD. It's not *exactly* closed.

CONNOR. You say your father made this?

GODARD. How dare you.

CONNOR. (*Attempting to move the drawer*) Don't you think it's a bit stiff?

GODARD. It just needs a bit of wax. (*GODARD peers into the open drawer, then reaches his fingers into the opening. He leans the chest forward; a sound of rolling comes from the drawer. CONNOR looks up at the sky.*)

CONNOR. Sounds like rain.

GODARD. Got it. (*In order to use both hands he releases the chest, which falls back upright. Again the sound of rolling, again CONNOR looks skywards, worried. GODARD looks at him with contempt.*) Are you just going to stand there? Push the chest this way. (*Slowly CONNOR stops looking up and goes to the back of the chest of drawers to lean it towards GODARD. Again the sound of rolling. CONNOR looks mournfully upwards at the sky.*)

CONNOR. Is it getting dark?

GODARD. What's the date?

CONNOR. June the twenty-second.

GODARD. The nights are drawing in.

CONNOR. Is it night yet?

GODARD. (*Still peering in at the opening.*) I couldn't say. There, I've got it. (*He pulls from the drawer a large white candle.*) That'll do the trick. (*Bent low, he begins to rub the candle against the sides of the drawer and closes it with his shoulder.*) Voilà.

CONNOR. Have you shut it again?

GODARD. I have.

CONNOR. After all that?

GODARD. Try it. (*He gestures towards the drawer, then places CONNOR's hands on the handle. Unconvinced, CONNOR grasps the handle with both hands and braces himself for a great effort. The drawer comes free with ease and CONNOR falls back, holding the drawer.*) See the quality of the workmanship. Those drawers were made to last.
(*Still lying on the floor, CONNOR examines the joints on the drawer with admiration.*)

CONNOR. Dovetails, that's quality. (*He taps the drawer. Places it on its end on the ground, then raises himself and sits down on it.*) So what are we talking about here?

GODARD. Let me wax the runners. (*He reaches into the space left by the drawer and rubs the candle along the two runners that sit either side of the drawer.*) She'll handle like a dream now. (*He steps back and gestures again to the opening.*) Try putting it back now.

CONNOR. (*Returns the drawer to the space and cautiously closes it.*) May I? (*A smug nod from GODARD. Delicately CONNOR opens the drawer then begins to fill it with the contents of his right-hand pocket, an enormous quantity of underpants, until the drawer is full to overflowing. He then leans his shoulder against it and closes the drawer with effort.*) Like a dream.

(*GODARD stands the candle in the middle of the chest of drawers and lights it with a match.*)

Curtain

ACT TWO

Scene as before. Light lower. The chest of drawers and the mound lit, fading to darkness elsewhere on the stage. The candle is still burning. CONNOR is kneeling before the chest of drawers, his hands moving over the drawer fronts as though searching for something.

CONNOR. I said I don't need your help. I can do this on my own. (*GODARD remains standing silent. He takes off his hat and looks inside it. Puts it back on his head and adjusts it. CONNOR's movements become more frustrated.*) Well, lend a hand. Lend a hand! Can't you see I need help? She's stuck fast.

GODARD. Try one of the other drawers.

CONNOR. I don't want to look in one of the other drawers. I want to look in the bottom drawer.

GODARD. It hasn't been opened in a long time.

CONNOR. What use is a drawer that can't be opened?

GODARD. For tidying things out the way. Like a memory you can't remember.

CONNOR. A memory you can't remember? Do you mean like time lost?

GODARD. Like dirt flushed down the pan.

CONNOR. What if somebody else remembers it?

GODARD. Not the same. Two people can't have the same memory.

CONNOR: (*Struggling still with the drawer front.*) Well, a drawer that can't be opened isn't a drawer.

GODARD. It did once. It was a source of great joy.

CONNOR. (*Pulling hard.*) This?

GODARD. Oh, how often she would sit looking into that bottom drawer. (*Pause.*) Fine linens, lacework, napkins. All embroidered by her own fair hand. Did you ever see such delicate fingers? What hopes were harboured in that little chest. The fine dinners that she planned, white tulips opening in spring sunlight as it falls across the lace-draped oak chiffonier. The hand-knitted jacket and booties lovingly fastened with a ribbon. What dreams dwelt in its lined and scented walls.

CONNOR. You've remembered.

GODARD. Who needs memories.

CONNOR. Happy memories.

GODARD. Most painful of all.

CONNOR. (*Still struggling with the drawer.*) You'll have to
   help me.
   (*GODARD falls to his knees beside CONNOR. They take
   turns alternately screwing the handle on at each side of the
   wide drawer. The handle is passed back and forth between
   them, opening the drawer an inch at a time, until the drawer
   is open.*)
CONNOR. Gogo. There's something in it. It might be
   something to eat.
GODARD. I don't think so. Let's close it. Before night falls.
CONNOR. (*Looking skywards.*) Night is falling?
GODARD. Falling quickly.
CONNOR. (*Leaning forward and reaching into the drawer*) Fine
   woollens. Delicate filigree of embroidery on fine cotton.
   (*Hopefully.*) There's a little bone, wrapped in muslin. A
   leg. (*Disappointed.*) There's not much meat on it.
   (*GODARD removes his hat and holds it with both hands
   against his breast.*) Material crumbling to dust. (*Slowly.*)
   Silken strands of hair. (*Pause. CONNOR removes his hat
   too and holds it over his chest.*)

Curtain

ACT THREE

Scene as before. Though darker, the chest of drawers is now partly buried so that the bottom drawer is no longer visible. CONNOR, crawling on all fours, pats the earth down. GODARD, standing, holds a shovel and uses it to do the same. The candle still burns.

CONNOR. Words fail me.
GODARD. There was nowhere else to put him.
CONNOR. Has night fallen yet?
GODARD. (*Looking up*) Nearly.
CONNOR. Are there stars?
GODARD. No.
CONNOR. Not one can be seen?
GODARD. (*He looks again*) No.
CONNOR. But they're there?
GODARD. If you say so.
CONNOR. I can smell them burning.
GODARD. It's the candle.
CONNOR. (*Looking up with hope*) Twinkling above?
GODARD. Sort of.
  (*CONNOR attaches the handle to the lowest of the drawers
  still visible. He pulls the drawer out from the chest, produces
  another candle from his pocket and waxes each side of the
  drawer, turning it upside down before pushing it partially*

back into the chest and sliding it back and forth testing its movement. He repeats the process with each of the remaining drawers, closing them each slightly further to create a set of steps.)

CONNOR. Will you help me up. (*He offers his arm to GODARD.*) I was going to say a prayer.

GODARD. (*Cheerily*) A prayer? Good God.

CONNOR. Tell me. I've been meaning to ask you. What keeps you from hanging yourself?

GODARD. She used to ask me that. After he ... Before she ... Before ... (*Pause.*) I've always been a late developer. (*He rises from his knees, takes CONNOR's arm and begins to climb the steps.*)

CONNOR. Watch the varnish! It'll come up nicely with a bit of beeswax. (*GODARD reaches the top of the chest, removes his hat and holds it across his chest in a statuesque pose. CONNOR meanwhile empties the contents of his left pocket, a pile of socks, onto the ground and begins tying them end to end.*)

GODARD. (*Abandoning his pose*) What are you doing?

CONNOR. (*Not pausing in his activity*) I'm making you a rope.

GODARD. With your stinking socks?

CONNOR. It won't be for long, I'll hang on to your legs.

GODARD. You'd do that for me?

CONNOR. You'd have done as much for me.

GODARD. That I would, Coco. Go on then, I'll have it as a scarf, it'll be cold up here.

CONNOR. Then you're not going to jump?

GODARD. I'll just keep watch (*Resuming the statuesque pose*) and wait.

Curtain

Unblocking a Sink

with Jean-Paul Sartre

Tools:
Plunger
Bucket
Wire
Cloth

Materials:
None

Monday 0700

Something has happened. So cunningly did it instil itself that at first I doubted my own senses. Even just now bent over the white hollowed form, I became aware of a slight feeling of awkwardness. The black and grey specks of hair shaved from my face float on the surface of the water, mixing at its edges with the residue of cheap soap to form a kind of scum or crust that attaches itself slowly to the basin as though drawn by some kind of residual magnetism.

Thursday 0800

The water level in the sink now descends so slowly it can scarcely be perceived by the eye, its movement can only be measured by the progress of the grey residue that coats itself onto the smooth white porcelain. Like the deposit of words and letters spawned by my pen, gathering without significance on the chalk-white paper.

Like a throat in paralysis, the sink will not swallow, it will not take any more of the filth that it has been forced to drink for so long. I look into the dark vent, straining my eyes to see what has fouled the pipe. Something glistens in the dark; the filmy surface of an eye, round and wet, is looking back at me. A foul smell emanates from the throat, an odour of sickness, nausea. I won't stand for it. I won't. The glistening surface disappears and the eye closes. There, in the filth it has come, the Blockage.

0900

Outside in the rue des Martyrs the shopkeepers are opening their doors, a group of men ending the night shift file into the brothel, their voices gargling and bubbling as they disappear one by one into the darkness of the interior. A woman emerges from the church. Dressed in black, she turns three times in a spiral before disappearing into the shadows of the narrow street that runs alongside the west wing of the church.

I leave the apartment to take my place in the ebb and flow. A bell rings and I hear the sound of shoes on bare floorboards, the smell of paraffin, paint, varnish. On the counter a small fleshy white creature lies on its back, its feet

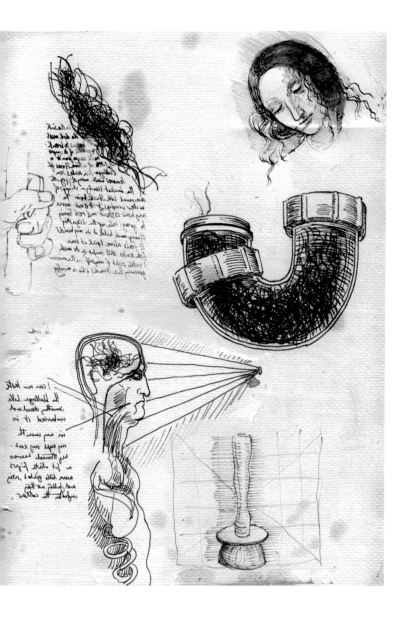

in the air in an attitude of submission. A second creature approaches, grasping an object in its paws. It appears to mount the first and as they brush against each other deposits something on its belly. The first rights itself and withdraws. A second bell chimes, the till is closed. I have paid. Brown paper rustles as it enfolds the awkwardly shaped object I have bought. The ironmonger, the same man who cut the key I had made for Anny before she left, hands me the irregular-shaped package. I see that the second of the creatures still hangs suspended in the air, it is my hand, it retreats to the dark warmth of my pocket where I feel its weight against my thigh.

Thursday morning in the Library

Things are bad, very bad. I cannot work. Every movement of my pen is without significance. My novel bores me. I have not energy even to fill my pipe. The object sits in front of me, where it draws the attention of the librarian. The Blockage has taken hold of me.

1630

Now unwrapped, the object sits on the counter next to the sink. A black hemisphere made of rubber, attached to a wooden handle. As though to reassure myself that it has not all been a dream, I run the tap and wait. There is no happy gurgling, no rush of water speeding down a pipe, to fall, unseen, as it passes through the apartments of the neighbours below. No, the water collects in the sink. I place the rubber dome over the plughole, block the overflow with a damp cloth and, using both hands, press down on the handle. The rubber hemisphere gives way and becomes a hemitoroid. It holds fast and I pull the stick back and forth, my arms jerking and flexing as the handle of the plunger moves like a piston in a cylinder.

My hands are shaking and the blood has rushed to my head. The plunger stands erect, dark water trailing over the bulbous rubber onto the counter. The plug still hangs by its chain from the tap, but the water level does not fall. The plunger does not work.

Beneath the sink there is a cupboard. Behind the mothballs and light bulbs, in the darkness beyond the scourers, cloths and washing powder, a white pipe forms the letter U. The letter brings to mind all that remains undone or has been reversed: Undone, Unloved, Unbroken, Undigested, Unforgotten, Unforgiven. Its two extremities are each attached by a threaded collar to a continuous pipe. My hands fumble in the dark space, loosening one of the collars. Already dirty water begins to seep from the broken seal. It trickles down the pipe to splash onto the packets of mothballs. As I come closer to the source of the Blockage my nostrils overflow with the putrid smell. The Blockage is everywhere.

I remove everything from the cupboard and place a bucket beneath the U-bend. I can now taste the Blockage. Like something dead and unburied it is in my mouth, my ears, my eyes. My stomach heaves. Fat white fingers move like grubs, rising and falling as they unfasten the collar. The little grooves of the thread show themselves one by one as the collar turns, like a needle on the surface of a record, bringing to life the voice of a long-dead singer. The U-bend comes away; water, putrid and grey, splashes onto my sleeve. I hold the U-shaped piece of plastic upside down; it is now an N-shape. The foul water pours into the bucket but nothing else emerges. The Blockage is still there, hiding in the bend. I am afraid to look. I do not want to see what has been growing in there, like a boil on the flesh until it is ready to burst. I am afraid. I am afraid of seeing again that viscous eye looking back at me. But I know I will look.

Slowly my hands bring the pipe towards me. The smell is overwhelming. Its extremities, now like two huge nostrils, blocked by a black horrible mass; vegetation that has crept up the drains from beyond the city limits, stretching its tentacles, its pincers, reaching closer into the life of the city that it seeks to reclaim. I push a piece of wire into one of the nostrils, pressing against the resistance of the Blockage, until it is forced from its nest and lands with a slap in the sink. Water oozes from the dark knot, I hear it drip into the bucket below. I reconnect the U-bend, tightening it by hand, and run the tap. The water lands in the sink, coating the surface, tracing a tangent, a curve, a spiral. The water thunders and the sink drinks and sings like a sailor, its thirst now unquenchable. The flow forms a continuum; if I run the tap long enough it will create an unbroken link between the reservoir and the sewage works, perhaps even a continuous loop, discontinuous only in respect of its filth. My intersection in this loop marks the point where the water becomes polluted, like my intervention in the life of Anny.

Under the force of the water the dark mass begins to break up, each of its components escapes a little at a time. Pieces of cabbage, fish scales, tea leaves wash away, leaving an animal-like nucleus of black hair swirling in the water. It is not mine, my hair is short and red turning to grey; it is Anny's. I take up the disgusting clump and hold it in my hands. It feels alive. I pick at the last of the fish scales still caught in its mesh. I catch sight of myself in the mirror, grooming the strands like a monkey. What am I doing?

1830

Night has fallen. Below in the street the lights are now on in the Café Mably. I throw the clump of hair into the waste bin, unfasten the chain to open the door and begin to descend the winding staircase. The sound of my steps echoes in the narrow stairwell. At the second landing the lights go out. I stand still, unable to advance, my eyes blinking in the darkness. The small white light of a spyhole shines out in the door before me and then grows dark. Someone is watching, waiting for me to move, but I cannot. I am the Blockage.

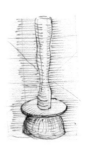

Painting a Panelled Door

with Anaïs Nin

Tools:
Screwdriver
Brush

Materials:
Primer
Undercoat
Gloss paint

She watched as he prised the lid from the paint, revealing the moonlike circle of white, into which he thrust the stiff animal bristle of his brush. His work was so sensual that women were attracted to him immediately. She had begun to court him, making little advances – talking about a lover in the past, or about the admiring glances she had received from the shopkeepers in the town. She lay back on the couch to watch him paint, her breasts thrust forward, her arms raised over her head. But the painter remained impassive; his passion found expression only in his work. Deep down she dreamed of a man who would rule her, take the lead sexually, yet the impassivity of the artist stirred her. Her admiration turned to love and she longed for him to make demands of her. When she looked at his strong hands and saw the paint beneath the nails, she yearned to feel their strength, to smell the perfume of turpentine and linseed rubbed onto her body, as he held her.

By night, as if in a dream, she walked the long corridors of the old hacienda, her body throbbing, as she sought the scent of fresh paint, eager to touch her fingers on its tacky surface. She was forced to become adventurous and bold. Each time she passed him at his work she brushed more closely by him, rejoicing to see the little flecks of paint smeared onto the smooth silk of her kimono. Finally she lost all reserve. Passing the painter in a doorway, she allowed her hand to brush against his brush. Suddenly he pushed her away, as if her gesture had insulted him. He looked proud, untouchable.

"What have I done?" she said.

"All this week you have watched me paint." His frown became a smile. "Now I will watch you." He handed her a brush, and pointed to the door that he had already stripped of its handle and brutally rubbed down earlier that day. "Paint."

Dressed in only her kimono, she now stood before the door, thrilling to feel the dark rectangle of stiff hair beneath her fingers.

"I said paint."

Observing her as she stood before him, he saw that she did not know how. Gently but firmly he directed her. Allowing her hand to be guided in his, she saw how the

sticky white paint clung to the dark hair as she dipped the little brush into the open pot and ran the bristles along the edges of each panel. "First you must paint the mouldings in all the panels." As she followed his instructions the wet bristles began licking paint into every crevice and ornamentation, flicking against each curve until the paint grew thin and viscous.

Behind her she could hear the breathing of the painter. He observed the contractions of her muscles as she reached high, squeezing the brush tightly. "More paint," he commanded, watching now how her hips pushed towards him, her head held low, as she recharged her brush from the little pot of paint.

"Don't stop," he said. At the sound of his voice she pressed her brush to the door and a spurt of white paint trickled onto the floor. "You are pressing too hard. Be gentle, the gentlest of pressure and the brush will respond. Too much and the brush will spill its load. Clean it up now, with the cloth and the white spirit."

Feeling her body vibrate with unsatisfied desire, she obeyed his every command. The odours of turpentine, paint, of pinewood filled her senses and through their smell, so strong and penetrating, she felt his presence.

"Now paint the panels. Do not dip your brush too deeply into the paint."

She began to understand the rhythm he required of her, her body swaying with the movement of her arm. She could no longer see the painter but she sensed his eyes on her back, tracing the contours of her body beneath the silk of the kimono. She felt every stroke of the brush as though its pure bristle were moving on the surface of her skin. Each movement in the paint created tiny currents and eddies, that she felt in her blood, watching as they disappeared in the paint, so wet, so inviting that she longed to touch it.

"When you have painted each panel stroke your brush along the grain." His breath came more heavily now and his voice fell lower in pitch. "Now to tackle the muntins." She imagined it to be a pet word of his, used for her breasts or thighs, and anticipated his strong hands taking her, but his long fingers pointed instead to the vertical pieces of wood at the centre of the door.

Now their breath kept time, little beads of sweat formed on her forehead and the painter's instruction grew more forceful; he seemed driven into a frenzy. "Next, the cross rails." He directed her hand to the three horizontal pieces of wood that helped to form the frame. "Here, *here* and HERE." His hair flew wildly as he swung his arms like the conductor of an orchestra. He seemed tireless and her arm ached with effort. What stamina he possessed, but she urged herself on, desiring only to give pleasure to her teacher, to give a good finish.

"Lay your brush against the stiles, the outer verticals that form the frame. You must work quickly, while it is still wet. Once it dries the bristles stick; it will leave the marks of the brush. Faster, faster."

With the last stroke she fell back, spent, her kimono lay open as her exhausted arm fell aslant her body, leaving a trickle of white paint across her flank.

The brush, she knew, would never tire, not until it had soaked up the last drop of paint. She lay trembling, her body naked, as the painter stood over her and uttered what she thought could not be possible. "Now is not the time to rest – you must clean your brush before it dries. For the second coat you will do it all again only with a better finish."

List of Illustrations

THE END